WHAT WOULD
Jefferson SAY?

WHAT WOULD

Jefferson SAY?

*What Our Third President Would Think of the
World Today—from the Budget Deficit and Race
Relations to Freedom of Speech and Family Values*

Garrett Ward Sheldon

A Perigee Book

A Perigee Book
Published by The Berkley Publishing Group
A member of Penguin Putnam Inc.
375 Hudson Street
New York, NY 10014

Copyright © 1998 by Garrett Ward Sheldon
Book design by Casey Hampton
Cover design by Charles Björklund
Cover illustration by Victor Juhasz

First edition: October 1998

Published simultaneously in Canada.

The Penguin Putnam Inc. World Wide Web site address is
http://www.penguinputnam.com

Library of Congress Cataloging-in-Publication Data

Sheldon, Garrett Ward.
    What would Jefferson say? / Garrett Ward Sheldon.—1st ed.
      p. cm.
    "A Perigee book."
    ISBN 0-399-52448-7 (pbk.)
    1. Jefferson, Thomas, 1743–1826—Political and social views.
2. United States—Politics and government—Philosophy. 3. United
States—Politics and government—1993–   4. United States—Social
conditions—1980–   I. Title.
E332.2.S545 1998
973.4'6'092—dc21   97-51818
                                              CIP

Printed in the United States of America

10 9 8 7 6 5 4 3 2 1

Contents

PREFACE   1

INTRODUCTION   2

ONE: *Balanced Federal Budget*   8

TWO: *The Military*   16

THREE: *Religion and Morality*   25

FOUR: *Race Relations*   36

FIVE: *Political Leadership*   47

SIX: *Family Values*   64

SEVEN: *The Economy and Welfare*   75

EIGHT: *Education*   84

NINE: *Health Care*   98

TEN: *Crime*   105

ELEVEN: *States' Rights*   112

TWELVE: *Freedom of Speech*   121

THIRTEEN: *Women*   133

FOURTEEN: *Drugs*   143

FIFTEEN: *Manners*   148

SIXTEEN: *Art and Architecture*   154

SEVENTEEN: *The Environment*   163

EIGHTEEN: *Science*   172

NINETEEN: *Entertainment*   196

CONCLUSION: *Jefferson's Hopes for America*   204

Preface

I recall pushing my chair away from the heavy wooden seminar table as the students filed out of the classroom of our Senior Seminar on Early American Political Thought. One remained behind. Joe Carico, a senior government major and president of the Student Government Association, posed an interesting question, proving once again that most of the best ideas come from college students. "Not to criticize your scholarly writing on Jefferson," he said tactfully, "but why don't you write a book on what Jefferson would say about today's issues, like the balanced federal budget, crime, and so on?"

I thought the idea was inspired, and couldn't get it out of my mind over the next several days. So, despite commitments to other academic publishers for different projects and work on the Russian translation of my first Jefferson book (*The Political Philosophy of Thomas Jefferson,* Johns Hopkins University Press, 1991), I began working on the "What would Jefferson say?" idea. This book is the result of that student's remark. I am grateful to him, now a law student, and to those others who shepherded it along; especially my literary agent, Jill Grinberg, for her insight and encouragement; my editor, John Schline, for his organizational brilliance and humor; and Rhonda Terry, for her careful preparation of the manuscript. Special thanks also to David Eastwood of Pembroke College, Oxford University. Any errors of insight or interpretation are mine alone.

Garrett Ward Sheldon
Pine Hill, Virginia

Introduction

"Jefferson still survives."

—JOHN ADAMS'S LAST WORDS, JULY 4, 1826,
THE FIFTIETH ANNIVERSARY OF THE
DECLARATION OF INDEPENDENCE, SHORTLY
AFTER JEFFERSON HIMSELF DIED

This book presents Thomas Jefferson's likely views on many contemporary American issues. From lively topics like "family values" and balancing the federal budget to less volatile subjects like art and architecture, this volume gives Jefferson's attitudes and how he might enter into today's debates.

This approach reveals several things. First, it shows the amazing relevance of Jefferson's ideas to our problems today. Some of his remarks are so timely that they sound like they were said yesterday in the *New York Times* rather than two hundred years ago. Quotes on subjects as diverse as multiculturalism, free speech, education, and manners still ring true. T. J.'s thoughts on women, race relations, and crime are so current that the latest books and controversies on them are reflected in his ideas. His concern with the deleterious effects of drugs on society, his interest in "holistic" health care, his belief in "virtue," and his love of the environment mirror much of contemporary opinion. Mr. Jefferson's fascination with science and inventions continues to be manifest in American technological development (what he would have done with the Internet!). Americans' concerns about the quantity and quality of entertainment are expressed in Jefferson's attitudes toward leisure.

Another consequence of comparing Jefferson's ideas on current issues with our own is often finding his ideology blending liberal and conservative solutions to today's dilemmas. For example, on the question of a balanced federal budget, Jefferson was conservative in wanting a lean federal government but liberal in expecting extensive public services in education, welfare, and even health care. His law in Virginia on "workfare" embodies principles of the latest state welfare reform programs. His attitude toward unfair international trading partners (in that day France and Britain rather than Japan and China) is remarkably similar to ours today. Jefferson even faced Arab terrorists who took hostages, demanded ransom, and threatened American interests abroad (the Barbary pirates).

On the popular family values debate, Jefferson adhered to the traditional standards of his day but experienced the failure to achieve that ideal throughout his life—losing his father early in his teens; raising his own children alone after his wife's early death; helping his daughters face domestic violence and the "single-parent household." A loving and devoted husband and father (and grandfather), Jefferson nonetheless sowed some wild oats before and after his marriage. He once tried to seduce a friend's wife (by naively slipping her romantic quotations from classical authors) and as a widower flirted with married women and may have kept a mulatto mistress. Most of his liaisons seem to have started when he was in France. . . .

Like many liberals today, Jefferson believed strongly in absolute freedom of speech and freedom of religion (and authored provisions in Virginia law that became models for the U.S. Constitution First Amendment rights). But like conservatives and many moderates, he thought that shared moral values were essential to American democracy and progress. He held overtly racist attitudes toward blacks, as Ken Burns's recent PBS series documented, but condemned slavery and exhibited tremendous guilt over the tragedy of race relations in America. He held traditional views on the proper relations between men and women but was legendary for his keen appreciation of women's sensitivities and talents.

Does this sound paradoxical? It is. This portrait of Jefferson through contemporary issues will reveal not only a timely and relevant figure but a complex, almost dialectical one as well. As Henry Adams described it, Jefferson's character could only be drawn "touch by touch with a fine pencil, and the perfection of the likeness depended upon the shifting and uncertain flicker of its semitransparent shadows." A picture emerges of an unusually gifted human being often brought down by human weaknesses that frustrate the realization of his highest ideals. A gentle, intelligent, urbane individual, as kind and interesting as anyone you'd like to meet, yet vicious toward his political foes (calling the Federalist administration a "reign of witches"). Aloof and private toward most of his common neighbors, yet friendly and attractive to the humblest of strangers. Wanting a leadership in the American Republic of "virtue and merit," yet dealing with all manner of questionable folks in the early Democratic Party. Able to converse with the lowest worker, yet elevated to the extent that President John F. Kennedy told a White House dinner of Nobel laureates that it was "the most extraordinary collection of talents . . . that has ever been gathered together at the White House, with the possible exception of when Thomas Jefferson dined alone."

That is also why around the world Jefferson is regarded as "the Prophet of Democracy" and why I've personally met scholars deeply interested in his political ideas in Russia, Turkey, India, and Britain.

Because this is meant as a popular book, I have decided (as Merrill Peterson did in his popular biography *Thomas Jefferson and the New Nation*) to forgo the "scholarly apparatus" of footnotes and bibliography, which for the most part is unnecessary for academic readers and a nuisance to general readers.

Despite a long American tradition of looking to the Founders for advice, some critics may actually question the validity of attempting to apply Jefferson's ideas to current issues, claiming either that it is impossible to deduce what someone who lived two hundred years ago would think of today's circumstances or that it's illegitimate and irrelevant to do so. As one columnist wag wrote of this practice earlier in this century: "what I'd like to know is what Thomas Jefferson knew about th' troubles iv ye an' me? . . . He was a good man in his day, though I don't know that his battin' av'rage'd be high again' th' pitchin' iv these times."

Taking the last complaint first, I think the ideas of the author of the American Declaration of Independence and leading political philosopher of the early Republic are highly legitimate and relevant to our contemporary social problems. He helped set up the system that frames most of them, so his theories continue to be important as long as we retain this system. Whether eighteenth-century notions can be applied to a very different twentieth-century world is a much harder proposition, but I still think it can be done. How? How can we say that some of Jefferson's notions would "change with the time" and others would not? I venture to say that were he alive today, Thomas Jefferson would not insist on wearing a powdered wig but that he would still believe it best to have a balanced federal budget. The powdered wig is part of fashion—trivial, transient fashion—and can safely be changed with the times. The balanced federal budget comes out of deeply held philosophical viewpoints (specifically, John Locke's belief in limited government and Aristotle's ideas on small-scale, local democracy) that Jefferson held as part of his personality and intellectual world. So, when a contemporary issue touches on not just the experience of Jefferson but the underlying logic of one of his belief systems (philosophical liberalism, classical natural law, Scottish moral sense psychology, etc.), we can safely say what he might think on an issue.

As you will see, Jefferson's opinions on education, abortion, criminology, evolution, and architecture don't just reflect the standards of his own time (in fact, at times he rejects those standards) but involve an underlying reasoning and logic. That makes it possible to apply the ideas and attitudes of America's favorite Founder to today's society. I promise that I did not rely on any séance, psychic, New Age channeling, or other sorcery. My knowledge of Jefferson's ideas comes from almost twenty years of study of his writings, environment, and philosophies. My application of Jefferson's eighteenth-century ideas to twentieth-century issues is informed by that study and is admittedly subjective.

In fact, this has been an American practice almost since the moment of Jefferson's death, as Professor Peterson showed in his book *The Jefferson Image in the American Mind* (Oxford, 1960). He argues that Jefferson's thought has cast a long shadow over Americans' image of themselves. From the Jacksonian Democrats who invoked Jefferson's "democracy of the people" to Theodore Roosevelt's application of Jefferson's continental expansionism to FDR's New Deal, T. J. has been the patron saint of American politics. If every generation of Americans defines itself by reinterpreting Jefferson's political thought, this work may be "Jefferson the Moderate." I don't know. This book certainly shows how President William Jefferson Clinton is "Jeffersonian" on some policies (see "The Economy and Welfare" chapter); but on others ("Political Leadership," "Women," and "Manners") Clinton is no Jefferson.

On the other hand, Newt Gingrich is no James Madison either, despite his penchant for quoting the *Federalist Papers*. The Republican Right may resemble Jefferson in its reduction of federal programs and encouragement of states' rights, but it defies T. J.'s concern with individual liberty from corporate tyranny. Jefferson would be as worried about assaults on citizens' rights from vast multinational empires, corporate interest, and bureaucratic fiat of all forms. The American insurance companies that operate nationally but are only ineffectively regulated at the state level, who routinely force consumers to accept "exclusion riders" (denying coverage over most critical illnesses), are only one example of "free enterprise" that Jefferson would regard as legitimate under public scrutiny. The popular (and subversive!) cartoon *Dilbert* reveals the threat to individual rights (and dignity) of recent corporate "restructuring" and "downsizing." Jefferson cared about the abuse of power by either public or private organizations, especially over the weakest members of society. My hope is that this book will be enjoyable, interesting, and stimulating on those subjects that Jefferson hoped Americans would always care deeply about.

One

BALANCED FEDERAL BUDGET

"I am for a government rigorously frugal."
—THOMAS JEFFERSON, 1799

Despite his attitudes on *public* frugality and a balanced federal budget, Jefferson didn't practice much *private* frugality and had a very unbalanced personal budget. By his late thirties, Thomas Jefferson was one of the wealthiest men in Virginia, with ten thousand acres on three plantations and 180 slaves. But a combination of extravagant living, lengthy public service, and strange accounting practices led him to be continually in debt and to die bankrupt.

Even without credit cards, Jefferson managed to run up the debt for such necessities as French wine, expensive clothes, an elaborate mansion, fine horses, thousands of books, and fancy carriages. The vagaries of the market in his chosen area of tobacco husbandry didn't help, but Jefferson's odd accounting system (he wrote down every day-to-day expense but knew nothing of debit/credit accounting—was frugal in small expenses but lavish in large ones) combined with extensive entertaining kept him living beyond his means most of his life.

Financial ineptitude combined with bad luck to finish off his estate at his death. As president, he spent $2,400 a year on wine for entertaining (about half his annual income). The economic depressions of the early 1800s lowered his land values, and a constant swarm of houseguests at Monticello drained his resources. The final blow came when a friend defaulted on a $25,000 loan for which Jefferson had cosigned. All of this meant that when Thomas Jefferson died, his estate went straight to his creditors. His daughter and ten grandchildren were thrown out of the family home at Monticello and would have been destitute had not the state legislatures of both South Carolina and Louisiana given her gifts of $10,000 each.

In the end, a comment by Jefferson's slave Isaac seemed most to characterize Thomas Jefferson: "He was only rich in his larnin."

Still, Jefferson would want a lean federal government, but extensive public services. He believed in a balanced federal budget, and as president he immediately began cutting the federal debt. As one of his biographers wrote: "In the Jeffersonian scripture, debt and taxes were public evils of the first magnitude. They drained capital from the mass of citizens, diverted it from productive enterprise, and supported a system of coercion, corruption and privilege . . ."

During his first term as president, Jefferson's primary fiscal goal was to extinguish the federal debt piled up by previous administrations. He accomplished this by greatly reducing federal government employees and the army and navy. In seven and a half years, Jefferson's administration trimmed the debt by $33 million, saving $2 million in annual interest on the debt. Despite extraordinary federal government expenses associated with the Louisiana Purchase and the Barbary Wars, Jefferson's administration reduced the total federal debt from $83 million to $57 million from 1801 to 1809. A British journal called it "the Millennium in government." Jefferson saw a large, expensive national government as a threat to democracy. History shows that rich, powerful central governments too easily become detached from the people, corrupt and despotic. And, for Jefferson, its debt causes high taxes. So, he said, "I am for a government rigorously frugal and simple, applying all the possible savings of the public revenue to the discharge of the national debt." The federal deficit doesn't just have negative economic consequences, it produces social and political burdens as well. He saw that "taxation follows public debt and in its train wretchedness and oppression."

Early in his career, Jefferson identified such a remote, expensive, and corrupt government with Great Britain. The "greed and avarice" of English merchants controlling Parliament led to the oppressive policies against the American colonies. Then, late in his career, he saw the "wealthy aristocrats" and American merchants tied to England as the source of political corruption in Washington, D.C. The Federalists' concentration of power in the central government reflected their centralized wealth elsewhere. And like the British mercantilist system, each hand washed the other. "Hamilton," Jefferson wrote, "was not only a monarchist, but for monarchy bottomed in corruption."

In both London and Washington, centralized power brought high taxes, oppressive government, and financial corruption—all of which poisoned the political virtue of states and localities. By removing the government from direct, close citizen accountability, the state was inevitably captured by venal commercial interests and self-serving aristocrats. The fiscal machinations of such an expensive, distant regime became for him a "detestable game" of "greedy creditors and speculators" manipulating the public trust and allowing "immense sums to be filched from the poor and ignorant." And Jefferson didn't even live to see the savings and loan scandal! Or DNC fund-raising techniques!

But Americans at times seem to want to have their cake and eat it too. They want, even demand, lots of public services (the elderly want Social Security and Medicare; parents want aid to higher education; businesses want government assistance and trade concessions; farmers want subsidies, etc.); but they don't want to pay for them with high taxes or deficit spending. High taxes rob us of money to spend on really important things, like videotapes and large-screen TVs, and the federal deficit screws up the economy with inflation and higher interest rates.

So how do we get realistic about this natural human tendency to want many things for nothing (which the federal government has been indulging for several decades)? One solution, for Jefferson, is moving domestic social programs back to the states and localities, where the visible "cause and effect" of more services costing more taxes provides a reality check, even for us Americans. World petroleum prices are a bit remote to most of us, but let the price of gasoline go up 0.5 cents at the local pump and listen to the outcry!

For Jefferson, by confining the federal government to international and interstate affairs, leaving most domestic affairs to the states, government will be most economical, responsive, and just. For he wants *extensive* public services, financed by taxes; but he wants them at the state and local levels, closer to the people, more sensible and effective:

> The way to have good and safe government, is not to trust it all to one, but to divide it among the many, distributing to every one exactly the functions he is competent to. Let the national government be entrusted with the defense of the nation, and its foreign and federal relations; the State governments with the civil rights, laws, police, and administration of what concerns the State generally; the counties with the local concerns of the counties; and each ward direct the interests within itself. It is by dividing and subdividing these republics from the great national one down through all its subordinations, until it ends in the administration of every man's farm by himself; by placing under everyone what his own eye may superintend, that all will be done for the best.

Jefferson advocates more public support for education, welfare, prisons, health care, and law enforcement than anyone of his time, but by those citizens *close to* the problem, sensitive to local needs, affected by their consequences. For example, one consequence of federal government micromanaging social programs in the states has been *mandating* a level of services, paid for by the state budgets, for things like Medicaid and a certain level of prison accommodations. As costs rise in those programs, states are forced to cut other state-funded programs to finance them: higher education, public libraries and museums, parks and recreation, etc. So the quality of life for average citizens goes down. By shifting responsibility for all state-run programs to the states, without mandates from Congress and federal judges, these social services can be better balanced.

For Jefferson, the closer the public program (and tax to pay for it), the more responsible it will be. Without such a state and local check on national government, he wrote, "Congress and Assemblies, Judges and Governors, shall all become wolves." But where each citizen is involved in some level of government, Jefferson thought, "he will let the heart be torn out of his body sooner than his power be wrested from him by a Caesar or a Bonaparte." He would be proud of Virginia today, where whenever a state legislator or governor suggests raising the state sales tax by a half-percent, a public outcry ensues and the proposal is quickly withdrawn.

And, like a conservative, Jefferson believes in private property and free enterprise, as the most fair, productive system of economics. A market economy rewards hard work, investment, and invention. If Thomas Jefferson had spent more time marketing his inventions (plows, clocks, hybrid seeds, and old bones) and not wasted so much time in public service, he wouldn't have died bankrupt! But like a liberal, he advocates progressive taxation to provide needed public services, giving the poorest among us equal opportunity and hope, and allowing the well-to-do to share a bit of their bounty. "Another means of silently lessening the inequality of property," Jefferson wrote, "is to exempt all from taxation below a certain point, and to tax the higher portions of property in geometrical progression as they rise." This principle, for him, would undoubtedly include capping the benefits of social entitlement programs (like Social Security and Medicare) for the very wealthy. To grant the same social benefits in public retirement and health care programs to those who can and those who cannot afford them is ludicrous. Or, at least, unfair. Foolish.

Jefferson advocates neither pure laissez-faire capitalism nor an absolute welfare state, but the "mixed economy" that is the secret of success in all Western democracies. The only arguments, for Jefferson, are over the balance of the mix. And that's what an intelligent citizenry should be debating, not wasting time making ridiculous statements about our opponents being "socialists" or "fascists," "compassionate" or "mean."

Jefferson would applaud the new Republican Congress's scaling back the federal government, returning public services to the states, cutting the deficit, and reducing taxes.

The Republican Party plan under the Gingrich-led Congress aims to shift much of the fiscal and policy responsibility for social programs to the states and localities. It also cuts several programs and departments, especially by reducing the expensive entitlement programs like Medicare and college assistance. With the graying of the baby boom generation, the capping of Medicare expenses is especially vital if other social programs are not to be lost, or taxes greatly increased, or the deficit sent orbiting around the moon. Ironically, it's the Republicans, the ol' "friends of the rich," the Millionaires' Club, that is capping Medicare benefits to the wealthy, making the rich pay for their own health care as they drift into dotage. The Democrats, "friends of the poor and downtrodden," the Robin Hood Club that likes to take from the rich and give to the poor, is resisting cutting benefits to anyone, even the rich! But there ya have it: politics makes strange sickbed-fellows.

Of course, Republicans want to translate these savings into tax relief for individuals, businesses, and families. By eliminating or "downsizing" many agencies (like foreign aid, farm subsidies, NEA, PBS, highway demonstration projects, military and federal employee retirement plans, and welfare), these congressional Republicans think we can lower taxes—giving Americans more money to spend as they see fit, or donate to Gingrich's reelection campaign.

But Jefferson, like Clinton and other liberal Democrats, would be concerned that needed social services be expanded by the states and not dropped altogether.

Clinton and the Democrats prefer fewer cuts in federal entitlement programs, slower movement to balancing the national budget, and using the savings for new federal programs. A memo from Office of Management and Budget Director Alice Rivlin detailed the "wish list" of new federal programs that could come from cutting other federal programs (including $50 billion in new infrastructure: a national information infrastructure system, a National Service Corps, fulfilling Educational Goals 2000, job training programs). Jefferson actually had his own wish list for federal infrastructure programs (including roads, canals, and education); the only difference is that he didn't want to institute it until the federal debt was paid off.

Again, Jefferson would agree with the conservatives' cuts only if their federal-government-bashing translated into increased state and local support for those programs eliminated at the federal level. He would like many of the intentions of the Democrats—he just wants them closer to the people, where they'll be more realistic, responsible, and sensitive to regional diversity.

On a balanced budget amendment to the Constitution, I think Jefferson would oppose it, but not for the usual reason that it would be too inflexible. Rather, Jefferson would want the democracy to become disciplined enough to balance the federal budget without the "strong arm" of a constitutional amendment. Resorting to such Draconian methods would, for him, be a sign of a failed democracy.

And while Jefferson would agree with much of the 1995 congressional Republican cause, The Contract with America, he would not have predicted many Americans' responses to it: cold feet. By fall of 1995, polls showed many Americans getting squeamish about the Republican federal budget cuts, and Clinton's popularity was rising as a consequence. By the time of the election, they still told their friends they like the Newt, then sneaked into the voting booth and pulled that long lever marked "Democrat." And that sly Neo-Pseudo-Crypto-Jeffersonian-Comeback-Kid Clinton was re-elected by a landslide. Wow. Of course, Jefferson was the guy who predicted we'd remain a nation of farmers and that in 1850 everyone would be a Unitarian!

Ironically, by the mid-1990s, the level of government spending at all levels (in relation to the GNP) was at its lowest in forty years. This would confirm Jefferson's belief that ideas matter. Despite the quarreling over government spending at the highest levels of Washington, the general public sentiment in favor of reductions has quietly been implemented.

Jefferson would approve.

Two

THE MILITARY

"Our militia are heroes when they have heroes to lead them on."

—THOMAS JEFFERSON, 1815

Like some other presidents, Thomas Jefferson never really served in the military. And he was at times accused of being a coward and a draft dodger as a result. This may be part of the reason President Clinton feels such an affinity for Jefferson.

Actually, Jefferson was a "colonel" of the Virginia militia, but that was largely an honorary title to a member of the gentry class. He hardly commanded any soldiers and was not directly involved in the Revolutionary War. Most of his war experience involved retreating from advancing British Redcoats.

He was later accused of cowardice for running away from Colonel Tarleton's British troops as they approached Monticello to capture him. Actually, Jefferson was wise to escape, since, as governor of Virginia, he could better serve his country *outside* a British jail. Or on a British gallows. The event occurred in 1781 when Jefferson, as the thirty-eight-year-old governor of Revolutionary Virginia, faced the invasion of three British army forces. As one biographer wrote: "this polite and thoughtful man found out, all too soon, that war played havoc with philosophy and the amenities." The legislature and governor had to escape first Williamsburg and then Richmond to avoid capture by the advancing British military. Most of Virginia's regular army was north of the commonwealth in George Washington's Continental Army. As the superior British force converged on Richmond, the Revolutionary government, governor, and legislature removed to Charlottesville ninety miles west to reconvene there. Lord Cornwallis dispatched Lieutenant Colonel Tarleton to Charlottesville with 180 heavily armed dragoons to capture the fleeing government and rebel Jefferson. Riding chiefly at night, they counted on the element of surprise to catch the Virginia legislators and governor (who was calmly writing official letters at his home at Monticello), effectively shutting down the new state government and humiliating the Revolutionary cause.

The British infantry covered seventy-five miles in twenty-four hours, an amazingly quick advance for the time. At a tavern named Cuckoo forty miles east of Charlottesville, one Jack Gavotte observed the British soldiers on the move and raced by horseback to warn the government. An enormous man and expert horseman, Jack rode on back trails and bypaths to beat the British to Charlottesville. Arriving at Jefferson's home near sunrise, Jack informed the governor of the British advance. Jefferson thanked him, gave him a fresh horse, and sent him into the town to alert the legislators.

The British dragoons headed up the mountain to capture Jefferson at Monticello. The governor had already sent off his houseguests to safety and then dispatched his wife and children in a carriage. Jefferson then calmly prepared his affairs and, looking through a telescope from his mountaintop home, saw British soldiers swarming all over Charlottesville. Mounting his favorite horse, he rode through the woods, over Carter's Mountain, and off to safety. A calm, deliberate, and brilliant escape.

But, late in life, Jefferson's political enemies used this incident to charge him with personal cowardice. Some in Virginia were ashamed at the continually fleeing "government." One woman wrote a letter at the time describing the "terror and confusion" of "Governor, Council, everybody scampering." "Our illustrious Governor," she continued, "took neither rest nor food for man or horse till he reached Carter's Mountain."

An inquiry into Governor Jefferson's official conduct was ordered by the Virginia Assembly. It exonerated him completely, ending with a resolution stating that "the sincere thanks of the General Assembly be given to our former Governor, Thomas Jefferson, Esq. for his impartial, upright, and attentive administration whilst in office. The Assembly wish, in the strongest manner, to declare the high opinion which they entertain of Mr. Jefferson's ability, rectitude and integrity . . ."

Still, as with other American presidents who have not served with distinction in the military, Jefferson's "flight to Carter's Mountain" dogged him with charges of cowardice the rest of his life. In a commonwealth that held military "honor" foremost in the list of public virtues, even the prudent escape could besmirch one's reputation.

But despite his less than exemplary military record, Jefferson would be for a strong military and national defense. "Weakness provokes insult and injury," he wrote, "while a condition to punish often prevents them." Further, Jefferson favored compulsory military service for all males: "We must train and classify the whole of our male citizens and make military instruction a regular part of collegiate education [ROTC!]. We can never be safe till this is done." Pretty militaristic there, Tom. So reinstatement of the draft would not bother T. J., and compulsory military or community service would appeal to him.

As president, Jefferson wished to balance the federal budget largely by cutting the military, but soon he found that was impossible, given the dangers around the world. European threats to American freedom and sovereignty demanded a strong army and navy. The world was not a friendly place—it was a brutal place—and American liberty and civilization needed defense, Jefferson found. Of the world conflicts begun by belligerent powers, Jefferson wrote, "some of them are of a nature to be met by force only, and all of them may lead to it." Negotiation was his preferred method of conflict resolution, but with some adversaries this was of little use. So his federal military budget included fortifying seaport towns, furnishing new gunboats, reforming the militia, building warships, and strengthening the army. President Jefferson deliberately backed up claims to justice and national interest with force.

One of the areas of international conflict where Jefferson defended American rights with military force was the Mediterranean region. For centuries, the Muslim states of North Africa (Morocco, Algiers, Tunis, Tripoli) had plundered trade ships sailing through that area. These Barbary pirates stole cargo and enslaved sailors, forcing them to work in hideous conditions, where many were subjected to torture, pestilence, and starvation. This ancient form of terrorism in the Middle East was compounded by extortion: the Barbary States demanded large sums of "protection money" from European traders traveling through the region, and when American ships began sailing there, they became victims of this piracy and extortion too. Unlike France and Britain, who simply paid exorbitant tribute to these terrorists, Jefferson proposed protecting American shipping with navy gunboats and retaliating on the Barbary States that attacked them (hence the verse in the Marines' anthem "to the shores of Tripoli").

While American diplomats were negotiating with the Moors, Algeria had captured two American ships off the cost of Portugal, demanding $1,200 for each of the twenty-one crew members. Jefferson had always considered dealing with such kidnappers futile and humiliating. No peace could be secure if based in "money for hostages." For him, a naval war would be less expensive and more effective in the long run. "Nor does it respect us as to these pirates only," he wrote, "but as to the nations of Europe." Jefferson insisted that "if we wish our commerce to be free and uninsulted, we must let these nations see that we have the energy" to defend ourselves.

Early on, Jefferson advised a confederacy of trading nations co-operating in forcing the Arab states to respect free trade (not unlike the multination force of Desert Storm). Blockading the Barbary ports and sinking pirate ships could be accomplished with a dozen frigates, he thought, since the Barbary States were comparatively weak and constantly torn by jealousies and strife with each other.

While Jefferson was president, he realized his plan against the Mediterranean powers. He sent the U.S. Navy to the Mediterranean to protect American shipping and respond to attacks from Tripoli. The Sultan of Algiers declared war on the United States by having the pole carrying the American flag cut down. Commodore Edward Preble blockaded and bombarded Tripoli. The American navy was reinforced—scarcely a single ship remained in American waters. Diplomacy backed by military might won a treaty in 1805, after four years of war. American commerce through the region was freed of tribute, piracy, and terrorism. Jefferson rejoiced over the victory. It was a blow not just against a brutal enemy but in support of free and secure international trade.

Internally, Jefferson would want America to have a lean but effective citizen army. The "militia" to him meant a "well-disciplined," trained, state force under the control of the state government. "A militia of young men will hold on until regulars can be raised, and will be the nursery which will furnish them," he wrote. Nothing, he said, could be more "distressing and disgusting" than an uncontrolled, vague militia. The so-called Modern Militia Movement does not resemble Jefferson's idea of a state militia. It is, instead, spread across thirty states and consists of an estimated 100,000 mostly lower-class and lower-middle-class white men in economic difficulty. Rural areas (like northern Michigan, Montana, Idaho) where farming, ranch, and timber industries are in decline and large portions of the population receive public assistance are breeding grounds for the Modern Militia.

The Modern Militia that bred the paranoid and destructive attitudes leading to the bombing of the Federal Building in Oklahoma

City shares almost none of the characteristics that Jefferson would identify with a healthy, vital militia. This Modern Militia is made up of men who have an extreme ideology of American democracy and impending Armageddon. For Jefferson, the militia would be most concerned about protecting the state from invasion; the Modern Militia Movement distorts this into an apocalyptic fear of the impending "one world order" under the Antichrist, using the United Nations and the federal government to impose the Beast of the Book of Revelation on America.

Besides the questionable biblical basis of this view (even most Fundamentalists believe that when the Beast or Antichrist assumes power and "the Tribulation" of the "Last Days" occurs, believers will have been swept away to heaven already), it gives this movement an ideological basis unlike any Jefferson expected. He may have considered the British "devils," but he subscribed to none of the millennial interpretations of eighteenth-century political events that were current in the colonies during the American Revolution. The excesses and violence of Oklahoma City are just what Jefferson would expect from the distorted view of the role of the state militia current in the Modern Militia Movement. In fairness, many of the Modern Militia denounced the Oklahoma City bombing. Norman Olson, commander of the Michigan Militia, said, "We have denounced the entire incident as an act of barbarity. It's totally alien to everything we believe. We are totally defensive. We do not engage in terrorism. We do not believe in answering the tyrant brutality with more brutality." Still, as the chapter on States' Rights will show, Jefferson would not accept the current National Guard view of the state militia, as a force based in states but under the control of the president.

On the related issue of gun control, Jefferson, like the Modern Militia, assumed the right of individuals, for self-defense and the basis of a state militia, to bear arms (own and use guns). Again, this assumed a largely rural, farming population. The city crime that has prompted calls for gun control was unknown by Jefferson, and I believe if known by him he would approve of reasonable local or state legislation regulating the sale and possession of firearms. But Jefferson would be suspicious of any *national* restrictions on guns, since that could be potentially oppressive. The need for gun control in New York City is different from that in rural Nebraska, so local and state jurisdictions should prevail.

On allowing homosexuals in the military, Jefferson adhered to the standard code of military justice that forbade it and would be surprised by those who advocate otherwise.

On homosexuality generally, when Jefferson began revising the Virginia legal code in 1776, he modified the penalty for sodomy: it had carried the death penalty, and he reduced it to castration. "Sodomy is a carnal copulation against nature, to wit, of man or woman in the same sex . . . ," he wrote. Jefferson would be surprised at Democrats' advocacy of allowing homosexuals in the military. Still, by today's standards, when even the most conservative commentators simply want to prohibit gays from the military, Jefferson's eighteenth-century penalty of castration would seem "cruel and unusual punishment."

Indeed, when Jefferson's revision of the Virginia code of laws was circulated in France a few years later, the literati found his punishments shocking, and he modified them. For bestiality, or having sex with animals, Jefferson eliminated all criminal penalties, asserting that its practice "can never make any progress" and its practitioners should be pitied rather than punished. Similarly, he removed the penalty of castration for rape, fearing that women might use the charge of rape to get even with men who rejected them. This view of women's psychology and their capacity for "vengeance" against unrequited love might also cause him to question the wisdom of mixing men and women in the military, as recent boot camp sexual harassment cases have confirmed.

The current debate in America over homosexuality is complex and difficult. Often, different sides on this important matter refuse to even hear the other's perspective—dismissing them as either "bigoted" or "perverted." Jefferson would bring a fresh breeze of rationality and openness to this discussion. Since homosexuals in eighteenth-century (American) society were not trying to assert their rights as a movement, it is impossible to find direct references in Jefferson's writings about gays or lesbians; but we can infer from his general views on science, law, and morals how he might respond to various perspectives on this issue.

The debate over rights of homosexuals and homosexuality has religious, scientific, and legal dimensions. Most antihomosexual Americans base their opposition to gays and lesbians on religious grounds: the Judeo-Christian Scriptures and traditions that reveal God condemning homosexual behavior (e.g., the destruction of Sodom and Gomorrah; Romans 1; 1 Corinthians 6:9; 1 Timothy 1: 10). Jefferson was at best a lukewarm Christian, openly declaring Unitarian sentiments later in his life. He edited a copy of the Gospels of the New Testament (thereby not including either the Old Testament or Paul's letters, which contain the severest condemnation of homosexuality) by cutting out all the miraculous and supernatural passages, leaving only the ethical teachings of Jesus. So we probably can't expect T. J. to use a traditional religious argument against homosexuality. Yet if he did, Jesus' statements that marriage was intended by God between a man and a woman, and his references to the destruction of Sodom and Gomorrah, would give little support to the pro-homosexual argument.

Often, the pro-homosexual community enlists scientific evidence for a genetic origin of homosexuality, arguing that such behavior is not a choice, but compelled by their biology, even "how God made them." In 1991 a scientist at the Salk Institute reported finding that a section of the brain (a bundle of neurons in the hypothalamus) in homosexual men is much smaller than the same brain section in heterosexual men. This led some to argue that homosexual tendencies are biologically determined, not a result of sinful and perverse lust or mental illness. Others in the scientific community contested this conclusion, pointing out that behavior can affect the physical structure of neurons and it is just as possible that a homosexual lifestyle changes those found in the brain. Jefferson's scientific bent would be intrigued by any physiological investigations explaining this condition and would probably be open to scientific evidence. But his scientific and medical investigations surmised that other negative conditions could be inherited (such as idiocy in monarchs), so that wouldn't necessarily jusify it for Jefferson.

Three

RELIGION AND MORALITY

*"I consider ethics, as well as religion, as supplements to
law in the government of man."*
—THOMAS JEFFERSON, 1824

Thomas Jefferson believed in the importance of religious morality
to American society, even if he didn't always live up to his own
high standards. He had a strong, personal religious faith that sustained him during times of tragedy and remorse.

He was, as one scholar wrote, a "pious and a regular church
attender who wrote very harsh criticisms of religion." Many "religious" people of his time called him an atheist and an infidel, but
he had a deep and abiding faith in God.

Jefferson was raised in the Established, or official, Church of
England in colonial Virginia. Also known as the Anglican Church
(now Episcopal Church), it was even then known for its sophisticated, liberal, and worldly qualities. The beauty and dignity of its
liturgy, sacred music, and church architecture gave Anglicanism an
aristocratic flavor. Its elegance and well-educated clergy made it
"the religion of the Gentleman," or as one wag put it: "The Anglican
Church is the House of Lords in prayer." Ralph Waldo Emerson,
traveling in England, noted the gentlemanly quality of Anglican
clergy. There was an urbane, intellectual quality to the church that

Jefferson grew up in, which affected his views of Christianity all through his life. The Episcopal Church that today ordains homosexuals to the priesthood was already, in the eighteenth century, a worldly and sophisticated institution. One joke about the Episcopal church (which I once knew well) was that their creed was "Through good taste ye shall be saved." A proud and elegant denomination. The prophet Jeremiah would have recognized it.

His upbringing in the Church of England gave a rational, worldly bent to Jefferson's religious faith, culminating in his conversion to Unitarianism later in life. None of St. Paul's "the wisdom of this world is folly to God." Jefferson's rational, even mathematical mind could not comprehend the mystery of the Trinity and couldn't "let go" to accept it on faith. Like doubting Thomas, Jefferson could not believe what he couldn't see—he was no mystic.

Yet Jefferson remained throughout his life a reverent believer in God, seeking his truth, confident in his providence, hopeful in his mercy.

Jefferson was an avid student of the Bible all his life, and his writings are salted with scriptural allusions and quotations. A clergyman who rode with Jefferson in a coach (not knowing his identity) found his discussion of religion so learned that he was sure Jefferson was a minister. One of Jefferson's earliest recollections was of being called upon as a boy to recite the Lord's Prayer before guests at dinner. Jefferson remembered his mother teaching him his prayers and his favorite sister, Jane, teaching him to sing the Psalms. As an adult, Jefferson usually read his compilation of the Bible before going to bed every night; he wrote: "I never go to bed without an hour's reading of something moral where on to ruminate in the intervals of sleep." By this he meant the Gospels of Jesus. Once, when tragic death struck his family, he was found alone in his room clutching the Bible. As he was dying, Jefferson uttered words like those of Simeon (Luke 2:29): "Lord, now lettest thou thy servant depart in peace."

Jefferson's Christianity stressed the Golden Rule and the Sermon on the Mount (Matthew 5–7; Luke 6). A God-given conscience, aided by reason, he believed, guides humans to the right path. Of the Gospels of Jesus, Jefferson wrote: "A more beautiful or precious morsel of ethics I have never seen." He created an edition of the Gospels, entitled *The Philosophy of Jesus,* that stressed the moral teachings of Christ. Jefferson's was a practical, activist religion, emphasizing personal repentance and good works. He wrote:

> The fundamentals of Christianity as found in the gospels are 1. Faith, 2. Repentance. That faith is everywhere explained to be a belief that Jesus was the Messiah who had been promised. Repentance was to be proved sincere by good works. The advantages accruing to mankind from our Savior's mission are these: 1. the knowledge of one God only. 2. a clear knowledge of their duty, or system of morality, delivered on such authority as to give it sanction. 3. the outward forms of religious worship wanted to be purged of that farcical pomp and nonsense with which they were loaded. 4. an inducement to a pious life, by revealing clearly a future existence in bliss, and that it was to be the reward of the virtuous.

Jefferson wanted religion to encourage good deeds, not pious pronouncements; he expected the Christian character to be known by its good fruits rather than its sanctimonious statements. A humble, gentle, kind, loving spirit; contrite, not arrogant. He rejected what he saw as the "mysticisms, fancies and falsehoods" of the apostle Paul, which Jefferson thought "distorted and deformed" the simple life and teachings of Jesus; but he would have concurred with St. Paul's description of Christian love (in 1 Corinthians 13) as patient and kind, not envious, boastful, or rude.

Dr. Benjamin Rush, Jefferson's lifelong friend, stated in his autobiography that Jefferson assured him that "he believed in the divine mission of the Savior" and that "he believed in the divine institution of the Sabbath" and "in the resurrection and a future state of rewards and punishments."

Such religious ethics could not be coerced, but could only emerge in an atmosphere of freedom. Forced conversions were, for Jefferson, not only false conversions, they were anti-conversions. For Jefferson, any compulsion in religion was contrary to the whole spirit of true religion. Jesus *invited* men to become his disciples; God left them free to accept or reject that invitation. So religion forced on the people by the state was contrary to true religion. "Almighty God hath created the mind free," Jefferson wrote in his Virginia Statute for Religious Freedom, and any legal coercions of an individual's faith "are a departure from the plan of the holy author of our religion." Jefferson's lifelong fight for religious freedom in America was to protect true religion from contamination by the state.

> *"Millions of innocent men, women, and children . . . have been burnt, tortured, fined, and imprisoned . . . What has been the effect of coercion? To make one half the world fools, and the other half hypocrites."*

Religious belief, for Jefferson, had to be voluntary to be sincere and genuine. "It is an error to believe that the operations of the mind . . . are subjected to the coercion of laws . . . The rights of conscience . . . are answerable . . . [only] to our God." This puts an awesome burden on the individual to seek out those truths to which he or she will be held accountable, and to religious bodies to share their knowledge of the Truth effectively, in the right spirit of humility. But for Jefferson, this life's quest works best in an atmosphere of freedom, where everyone is able to profess his or her own beliefs, and hear those of others. As Jefferson wrote in his law for establishing religious freedom in Virginia: "All persons shall have full and free liberty of religious opinion . . . All men shall be free to profess . . . their opinions in matters of religion." For Jefferson, in a democracy everyone should be free to believe, investigate, and express his or her own religious views. (Ironically, while many "religious" people of his time thought Jefferson's ideas of freedom would lead to the end of the church, they actually led to one of the greatest religious revivals in American history, called the Second Great Awakening.)

For Jefferson, a healthy religion didn't require state sanction, just liberty. The important thing was not to hinder a move of God by restrictive laws on religion. In this sense, Jefferson wanted a religiously neutral state—one that neither supports nor discourages religion (as the First Amendment to the Constitution aptly puts it: neither respects the establishment of religion nor prohibits the free exercise thereof). For Jefferson, this is not merely for the benefit of a secular government; the other loser in church-state entanglement is faith, which is invariably corrupted and demeaned by close association with worldly power. Jesus informed the Roman governor Pontius Pilate, "My Kingdom is not of this world." Jefferson was a deeply spiritual person and resisted the corruption of pure religion by political motives.

Consequently, Jefferson was ecumenical all his adult life, supporting and frequenting churches of all denominations. He was baptized and married in the Episcopal Church and served on its vestry; he attended services at a Baptist church and he helped found the Calvinist Reformed Church in Charlottesville. He even attended some camp-meeting revivals in Virginia and contributed money to their collections. Captain Edmund Bacon, the general overseer of Monticello for twenty years, wrote:

> Mr. Jefferson never debarred himself from hearing any preacher that came along. There was a Mr. Hiter, a Baptist preacher, that used to preach occasionally at the Charlottesville Courthouse . . . Mr. Jefferson nearly always went to hear him . . . I remember his being there one day in particular . . . After the sermon there was a proposition to pass around the

hat and raise money to buy the preacher a horse. Mr. Jefferson did not wait for the hat. I saw him unbutton his overalls, and get his hand into his pocket, and take out a handful of silver. I don't know how much. He then walked across the Courthouse to Mr. Hiter and gave it into his hand.

As president, Jefferson helped the Catholic Church to be allowed to purchase land in the District of Columbia. He attempted to move the entire faculty of Calvin's University of Geneva to form the new University of Virginia! He encouraged funding clergy salaries and mission schools to Native Americans. But perhaps Jefferson's most famous ecumenical statement was about the cooperation of the different denominations in Charlottesville, where they shared the public courthouse for worship services. In 1822 Jefferson wrote to Dr. Thomas Cooper:

> In our village of Charlottesville there is a good deal of religion, with only a small spice of fanaticism. We have four sects, but without either church or meeting house. The Courthouse is the common temple, one Sunday in the month to each. Here Episcopalian and Presbyterian, Methodist and Baptist, meet together, join in hymning their Maker, listen with attention and devotion to each other's preachers and all mix in society with perfect harmony.

A few years later when each denomination built its own church building, Jefferson contributed money to all. His account book of 1824 shows "to the building of an Episcopal church, $200; a Presbyterian, $60; and a Baptist, $25."

Jefferson's ecumenical sentiments and belief in the need for freedom of religion would extend to our more religiously diverse America in the twentieth century. Now it is not just four different Christian denominations, but thousands of denominations and many non-Christian faiths. Jewish settlers were the only non-

Christian religious group in Jefferson's time; now Muslim, Hindu, and other religious groups have increased the pluralism of American religion. Jefferson's insistence on freedom to believe and profess one's religion would remain today. Yet he would still hope that the discussion of different faiths would distill the simple ethical teachings of Jesus—love, repentance, and forgiveness—that Jefferson felt were essential to a healthy, civilized democracy.

For Jefferson, democracy and religious freedom went hand in hand. Contrary to the medieval view that certain families or classes were chosen by God to rule over others, Jefferson insisted that our Creator (to use the term in the Declaration of Independence) endowed all individuals with a conscience, a moral sense, and natural rights to exercise it. "All eyes are opening," Jefferson wrote in his last letter before his death "to the rights of men . . . The mass of mankind has not been born with saddles on their backs, nor a favored few booted and spurred, ready to ride them legitimately by the grace of God."

Such God-given rights placed enormous responsibilities on individual humans and on nations, for Jefferson. All would be accountable to God for how they used their gifts and talents. Contemplating with horror the divine punishment on America for the sin of slavery, Jefferson wrote, "Can the liberties of a nation be thought secure when we have removed their only firm basis, a conviction in the minds of the people that these liberties are the gift of God . . . I tremble for my country when I reflect that God is just; that his justice cannot sleep forever . . . The Almighty has no attribute which can take side with us in such a contest."

For Jefferson, individuals and nations will be judged by God. And a nation that sanctions the enslavement or destruction of human life is liable to God's "wrath." This was particularly the case for America, in Jefferson's mind, because we had received so many blessings from God. God's providence has uniquely overseen America's settlement, freedom, prosperity, and growth. Jefferson's public speeches were filled with references to "that overruling Providence which governs the destinies of men and nations" and which "watches over our country's freedom and welfare." Comparing the United States to ancient Israel, Jefferson wrote: "the Being in whose hands we are, who led our fathers, as Israel of old, from their native land and planted them in a country flowing with all the necessaries and comforts of life . . . covered our infancy and His wisdom and power [guided] our riper years." Jefferson prayed that God would "enlighten the minds" of America's leaders and "guide their councils."

As one scholar wrote, Jefferson's political philosophy rested on his moral and religious thought. His personal motto, with which he sealed the wax on all his envelopes, "Rebellion to Tyrants Is Obedience to God," was borrowed from the book *Lex Rex,* by Scottish Presbyterian minister Samuel Rutherford. Consequently, Jefferson would applaud the moves in America to instill greater moral values in our schools, homes, and businesses. But he would be wary of those groups that advance a narrow or sectarian approach to reviving religious ethics in our country. Self-righteous reforms of the Left or Right would repulse him. For example, open school prayer except in a purely homogeneous local population (e.g., all Jewish, Christian, or Muslim) would be too narrow and sectarian to avoid mixing church and state. And Jefferson might note that the Supreme Court has never forbidden *silent* prayer by anyone in the public schools (a common occurrence during exam time!).

Jefferson believed that humans have a "moral sense," a conscience, that tells us what is right and what is wrong. This causes us to sympathize with the sufferings of others—to encourage and help them. It also causes us to recognize evil in ourselves and to check us in doing bad things. The moral sense, Jefferson said, is "the first excellence" of a virtuous nation. And happiness follows virtue. He told his young ward Peter Carr, "If you ever find yourself environed with difficulties . . . out of which you are at a loss how to extricate yourself, do what is right . . . Though you cannot see, when you take one step, what will be the next, follow truth, justice and plain dealing . . . [because] intrigue . . . chicanery . . . dissimulation . . . increases the difficulties tenfold."

Religious ethics inform that moral sense, and practice strengthens it. So Jefferson advised his nephew to be "good, learned and industrious," which would make him "precious to your country, dear to your friends, happy within yourself."

Virtue ultimately equals happiness, both individual and social. A wicked, depraved nation cannot be content, for Jefferson. Looking at the social decay in America, he might agree with the Psalmist, King David, that "the nations that forget God . . . shall be turned into hell" (Psalm 9:17). Since 1960, the violent crime rate in the United States has increased 500 percent. Illegitimate births have increased 400 percent. The teen suicide rate has tripled; the divorce rate has doubled. Alternative lifestyles contrary to four thousand years of Judeo-Christian civilization are abounding. Since 1972, over 30 million unborn children have been aborted. In a schoolteachers' survey of the top problems they faced in 1940 were gum chewing, noise, running in the halls, and littering; in 1990 they were drug abuse, alcohol, pregnancy, suicide, rape, and assault.

But virtue is best taught in freedom. Jefferson regards the Christian ethics of love, forbearance, and forgiveness as "the most sublime and benevolent code of morals which has ever been offered to man"; but no church or group has a monopoly on those ethics. Freedom of religion is the best means of sifting out those essential values and teaching and inculcating morality.

By allowing the full expression of religious ethics, Jefferson thinks the truest morality will be taught and spread. Even in the public sphere. He would agree with recent Supreme Court rulings allowing religious study and expression in public schools, as long as all groups are allowed to have their own meetings. He would object to those attempts to use the state to restrict or repress individual religious expression.

"Almighty God hath created the mind free . . . all attempts to influence it by . . . civil incapacitations . . . are a departure from the plan of the holy author of our religion . . ."

Jefferson encouraged the presence of religious institutions at the University of Virginia, saying, "It was not to be understood that instruction in religious opinion and duties was meant to be precluded by the public authorities . . . On the contrary, the relations which exist between man and his Maker . . . are the most interesting and important to every human being . . ."

The healthiest religious institutions, for Jefferson, exist in a free environment. And the healthiest nation is the one with the best morals. Ergo, the healthiest country follows from religious freedom. Liberty.

Thomas Jefferson's personal life displayed many of his ethical beliefs. He summed up his moral system as "to be grateful, to be faithful . . . to be open and generous," and he lived these principles. His granddaughter remarked on "the scrupulous fidelity with which he discharged the duties of every relation in life." Friends testified to his kindness, generosity, and forbearance. He regularly attended churches of all denominations, and before going to bed each night, he would read some moral book, "where on to ruminate in the intervals of sleep." He loved sacred music and filled his parlor at Monticello with paintings of religious scenes.

In the end, Jefferson would want to judge those who profess a concern for American morality by the moral conduct in their personal lives. (Does William Bennett live his *Book of Virtues*? Or does his manner discredit those virtues?) Do they love their families, show respect to friends and opponents alike, practice charity of feeling to all, and mercy to strangers? Do they "love the sinner" even while hating the sin that destroys them? Do they revere God more than worldly honor, wealth, and prestige? Are they arrogant hypocrites, self-righteous, boring? Or humble, loving, joyful, and interesting?

Jefferson himself would not measure up to his own high standards of morality as the chapters ahead on family values and manners will show. He would admit that.

Maybe that's why, late in his life, he hoped most for a merciful God . . .

RACE RELATIONS

"We have the wolf by the ears, and we can neither hold him, nor safely let him go."

—THOMAS JEFFERSON, 1820

Race relations in America, especially between African Americans and whites, have been the source of more social conflict than any other social problem: economic class, religion, or gender. From slave revolts and lynchings in the antebellum South to the L.A. police beating of Rodney King, the murder trials of O. J. Simpson, and controversies over affirmative action, racial tension has been a persistent feature of American life for the past three hundred years. Abraham Lincoln once said that it may continue until every drop of blood shed during the American slavery era was avenged. Jefferson wasn't quite that pessimistic.

Thomas Jefferson was a product of the slave-owning American South, and his problems and attitudes toward blacks reflect that social setting. His advice on racial tension is colored by his social background in the Virginia gentry class. Its racism is not very useful to us today, but his struggles, guilt, fear, and hopes are at least understandable to late-twentieth-century Americans, as we face the stubborn problem of racial justice and social harmony. Just as Jefferson hated slavery, but knew not how to get out of it, most Americans hate the continuing suspicions and tensions between black and white Americans, but don't know how to get around it, don't know how to solve these persistent problems. Progress has been made in greater racial tolerance, respect, and cooperation, but flareups of violence and mistrust show that we have a long way to go. Jefferson's own relations with African Americans and attitudes toward blacks and slavery may help us to understand this problem better and advance positive solutions.

Thomas Jefferson's earliest memory as a child was of being carried on a pillow by a black slave when his family moved from one Virginia plantation to another. One might say black slaves carried him for the rest of his life, and then carried him to his grave at age eighty-three. The approximately two hundred slaves owned by Jefferson built his elegant manor house, kept his fields of tobacco and cotton, nursed his children, cooked his meals, groomed his horses, and provided him with the vast leisure to become the cultured, educated, refined Virginia gentleman that he was famous for and to make the political impact he made on America and the modern world.

Jefferson was known for his humane treatment of his slaves. He would not countenance the common practice of beating or whipping those who were disobedient. He would not allow them to be driven or overworked. Rather, Jefferson employed modern management methods of material incentives and rewards to encourage the slaves to work harder, saying that he "loved industry and abhorred severity." He provided amply for their food, clothing, and shelter. He took care of them when they were sick or too old to work. A Monticello resident wrote that Jefferson's slaves regarded him as "one of the greatest . . . best men and kindest of masters," and a plantation overseer at Monticello said Jefferson was "always very kind and indulgent to his servants. He would not allow them to be at all overworked . . ."

Jefferson's personal boyhood slave, Jupiter, was more like a brother to him—his constant companion and friend, accompanying him to college and serving him faithfully. Only one incident of Jefferson being angry with Jupiter is recorded: when the slave allowed some other servants to use a horse that T. J. had instructed to be given a rest. Otherwise, he adored Jupiter and mourned his early death from illness and a poisoning witch-doctor treatment. He once chastised his young grandson for being rude to a black man they encountered on horseback, when the slave bowed and lifted his hat courteously and the boy didn't return the gesture. Jefferson said, in effect, to the lad: "That Negro is more of a gentleman than you are!"

From all evidence, the slaves on Mr. Jefferson's estate returned his affection with effusive love and loyalty. One Christmas, as Jefferson's carriage approached the house, the slaves greeted their master with exuberant joy; a witness wrote: "They collected in crowds around it and almost drew it up the mountain by hand . . . When the door of the carriage was opened, they received him in their arms and bore him to the house, crowding around and kissing his hands and feet." The writer of this episode of spontaneous affection of the Monticello slaves for their long-absent master presents it as a genuine, sincere, and natural display of love for Jefferson, a kindly master in a horrible social institution and tradition. Perhaps for this reason—the love and loyalty of blacks even under slavery—Jefferson felt tremendous guilt over his role in their enslavement. He wrote:

> Can the liberties of a nation be thought secure when we have removed their only firm basis, a conviction in the minds of the people that these liberties are a gift of God? That they are not to be violated but with his wrath? . . . I tremble for my country when I reflect that God is just; that his justice cannot sleep forever . . . The Almighty has no attribute which can take side with us in such a contest.

Jefferson knew that the consequences of the sin of slavery would be grave and severe on America. And they still are today.

So Thomas Jefferson hated slavery. He called it an "abominable crime," a "political and moral evil," and a "hideous blot" on America, caused by "avarice and evil." Yet he owned black slaves all his life, living off their labor and holding racist views on blacks' abilities. He meant it when he wrote, "I tremble for my country when I reflect that God is just." He knew the crime of slavery would inflict evil and suffering on Americans for generations, and he dreaded it.

Was Jefferson a vile hypocrite? A fool? An idiot? Or just human? Hundreds of articles have been written condemning, ridiculing, berating, and trying to explain Jefferson on this issue.

Jefferson himself tried to reconcile these contradictions by advocating the freeing of black slaves and their gradual relocation, repatriation, to Africa. He didn't think they could become productive citizens in the United States because he felt they were inferior to whites in reason and imagination. Jefferson believed blacks would long remember the abuse they had suffered under slavery, and many would want to retaliate. Violence would result.

Jefferson was deceived by the popular eighteenth-century "scientific" idea that Africans were inferior to whites, and even a different species from humans. The anthropology of his day claimed that blacks were a race between apes and men. "I advance it, therefore, as a suspicion only, that the blacks, whether originally a distinct race, or made distinct by time and circumstances, are inferior to whites in the endowments of body and mind." This racist view, Jefferson asserted, was bolstered by deficiencies in blacks' abilities in reason and imagination. "Comparing them by their faculties of memory, reason, and imagination, it appears to me that in memory they are equal to the whites; in reason much inferior . . . and that in imagination they are dull, tasteless, and anomalous." From his experience with the blacks on his estates, Jefferson claimed that their imagination was "wild and extravagant," that it "escapes incessantly from every restraint of reason and taste . . .

leaves a tract of thought as incoherent and eccentric as is the course of a meteor through the sky." (And Jefferson never even heard a speech made by Jesse Jackson!) But, almost apologetically, he insisted this was only a "suspicion." He was secretly ashamed of his racism.

The supposed lack of refinement in rationality and thought of blacks led Jefferson to repeat a common southern prejudice about Negroes—that they slept a lot. "In general," he wrote, "their existence appears to participate more of sensation ["feeling," "emotions"] than reflection. To this must be ascribed their disposition to sleep when abstracted from their diversions, and unemployed in labor. An animal whose body is at rest, and who does not reflect, must be disposed to sleep of course." This comparison of blacks' behavior to that of dogs or cats adds insult to injury. In similar racist style, Jefferson claims blacks have musical "rhythm" but not higher appreciation of complex music. "In music," he wrote, "they are more generally gifted than the whites, with accurate ears for tune and time," but "whether they will be equal to the composition of a more extensive run of melody, or of complicated harmony, is yet to be proved." He didn't live to see the many complex jazz and even classical musical works composed by black musicians in the twentieth century, or to appreciate the importance that black spiritual and folk music would have in the jazz age in America and throughout the world.

Jefferson belittled blacks' bravery in combat, attributing it more to lack of forethought than genuine courage. "They are at least as brave [as whites], and more adventuresome. But this may proceed from a want of forethought, which prevents their seeing a danger till it be present. When present, they do not go through it with more coolness or steadiness than the Whites." Not surprisingly, for this and other, more urgent reasons, Thomas Jefferson opposed Alexander Hamilton's plan of arming blacks during the American Revolutionary War.

Like many southern planters, Jefferson complained that black slaves showed a propensity to steal things (bits of food from the kitchen, household utensils, pieces of cloth); but unusually, he did not think this meant that they lacked integrity or honesty: "Notwithstanding these considerations which must weaken their respect for the laws of property [i.e., their enslaved condition], we find among them numerous instances of the most rigid integrity and as many as among their better instructed masters, of benevolence, gratitude, and unshaken fidelity." Jefferson observed many of the sweetest moral and emotional qualities in blacks—their affectionate and gentle disposition.

Still, Jefferson at times expressed doubts about blacks' inferiority. Corresponding with the black mathematician Benjamin Banneker, Jefferson expressed the belief that blacks' intellectual weakness might be due to their degraded condition under slavery and that after "a few generations" of freedom and opportunity, they would show equal abilities and accomplishments.

Time has proved this to be true, as American blacks of intelligence and skill rise into more and more positions of prominence and influence in our society. An *Ebony* magazine article, "30 Leaders of the Future," included young blacks in prominent positions in government, law, business, and religion. Another *Ebony* piece, "100 Most Influential Blacks," included General Colin Powell (former chair of the Joint Chiefs of Staff and featured speaker at the Republican Party National Convention in 1996); Federal Communications Commission member Andrew Barrett; world-renowned athlete Michael Jordan; the president of the National Baptist Convention; the mayors of Baltimore, Detroit, Denver, Birmingham, Cleveland, Minneapolis, Seattle, St. Louis, Atlanta, and Kansas City; several federal judges; congressional representatives; the chief justice of the Pennsylvania Supreme Court; the presidents of the National Dental Association, the National Newspaper Publishers Association, and the National Alliance of Postal and Federal Employees; and director of the Centers for Disease Control and Prevention. Now the secretary-general of the United Nations! I think even Jefferson, with his eighteenth-century Virginia gentry prejudices about blacks, would be convinced that African Americans have proved themselves equal to Euro-Americans in reason, imagination, and hard work. It would increase his fundamental belief in the improvability and equality of man.

So Jefferson would have agreed with affirmative action's attempts to raise blacks up from past degradation, even giving them advantages over whites for a while. But after "a few generations," seeing their accomplishments and successes, Jefferson would want blacks to stand on their own. He would agree with current efforts to eliminate favored conditions for blacks legally (like Governor Pete Wilson's abolishing affirmative action in California).

Jefferson would not be surprised by continuing racial tensions in America. He said: "Deep rooted prejudices . . . by whites; ten thousand recollections by the blacks, of the injuries they have sustained; new provocations" will continually aggravate racial conflict.

The American public response to the O. J. Simpson murder trial is emblematic of the continuing racial suspicion and division in this country. The *Newsweek* article on Americans' reaction to the "not guilty" verdict in the criminal trial opened with a photograph that spoke a thousand words. Gathered around a television screen is a group of two dozen college students, black and white, watching the jury announcement of the verdict. Captured in the photograph are the facial expressions of these educated young Americans at the moment their faces register the emotions flowing up from that jury decision. A white girl looks stunned, a white man angry, black women cheer, another white woman looks shocked with hands covering her face, a white boy seems puzzled, black men grin. A picture of social division, symbolic of the checkered racial past in America. The *Newsweek* poll taken right after the Simpson criminal jury verdict showed that 85 percent of African Americans agreed with the verdict, while only 56 percent of whites agreed that O. J. was innocent; 80 percent of blacks thought the jury was fair and impartial, while only 50 percent of whites thought it was unbiased.

Many blacks cheered at O. J.'s acquittal less for that particular verdict than for the fact that the United States court system could let off any black man accused of killing a white woman. Legal scholar Lani Guinier expressed this when she said, "The rejoicing is not that somebody got away with murder, but that somebody beat the system." Fourteen percent of blacks told *Newsweek* that they have more confidence in the American judicial system now. Thirty-seven percent of whites say they have *less* confidence in it. A large number of white Americans were outraged over what they saw as a mockery of justice, a kangaroo-court circus that ignored the obvious and allowed a wife-beating monster who'd committed a grisly double murder to go free.

On the World Wide Web a posting read, "I do not trust blacks now. They have proven that they are worse racists than any whites." Some commentators believe that the subsequent "legal backlash" against welfare, affirmative action, and other government programs that disproportionally help minorities was the consequence. The sight of American blacks uncritically celebrating the acquittal of a black person simply because he is black aggravated even liberal whites who traditionally favored public assistance to the disadvantaged. One white liberal said, "Why is the problem *always* the job or the schools or the police? Why is the problem *never* because 'one of us' did something wrong?"

But blacks who remember three hundred years of slavery, a hundred of segregation, and only thirty of social benefits still saw the system "rigged" against them. A group of black Howard University Law School students screamed and danced with joy at the O. J. acquittal verdict. In Harlem and the black Potrero Hill section of San Francisco, crowds poured out into the streets to celebrate, shouting and honking horns. Whites viewing this recoiled in horror and fear: how could people take pleasure in two mutilated murder victims and their grieving families?

This reveals the depth of difference in black and white Americans' perceptions. "This is accelerating America's descent into a state of psychological apartheid," said Rev. Eugene Rivers of Boston's black Azusa church. Yet the *Newsweek* poll showed 25 percent of American blacks believed Simpson *was* guilty. "I cringed at those scenes of jubilation," black Mayor of Kansas City Emanuel Cleaver said, "not because I didn't know how black people felt, but because of the fear and misunderstanding it would generate." Some blacks expressed dismay over a miscarriage of justice but said they were afraid to discuss it for fear of going against the "black cause" in this country. Even the subsequent "guilty" verdict in O. J.'s civil trial and high punitive damages didn't resolve the conflict: most blacks saw it as excessive and unfair, while many whites thought justice still had not been done.

Most of us find it painful to remember this episode of American social history; I find it hard to write about. But it shows the horrible suspicion and hatred and resentment between blacks and whites in the United States, which Jefferson predicted. It's so frustrating. The real culprits are the few southern planters and northern shippers who brought the first African slaves to Virginia. The rest of us have been living with, entangled in, the injustice of that act ever since. Yet ignoring it because it is unpleasant won't make the reality of racial tension in America go away. Fear pervades both sides, and reason and sympathy don't work too well in an atmosphere of fear.

Andrew Hacker, author of *Two Nations*, wrote, "We [whites] have a protocol on how blacks should behave. There are good blacks like Colin Powell, iffy ones like Jesse Jackson and bad ones like Farrakhan." American blacks resent such classifications and counter with Bill Tatum, editor of the *Amsterdam News*, that "three quarters of white America—including lawyers—reacted like spoiled children, saying the system did not work the way they wanted it" in the O. J. trial. With nearly one-third of black men in their twenties in prison or on parole or probation, and 90 percent of drug-related convictions involving blacks or Hispanics, many minorities share Tatum's dictum that "cops are crooked until they prove they're not." DeLores Tucker, the first black to serve on the

Philadelphia zoning board, relates an incident in which her husband was unfairly accused of stealing someone's wallet in a store because he was the only black man in the place. Such daily humiliation has hardened many American blacks into a tough cynicism. Ben Stein's remark rings true to this cynicism: "When O. J. gets off, the whites will riot the way we whites do: leave the cities, go to Idaho, or Oregon or Arizona, vote for Gingrich . . . punish blacks by closing their day-care programs and cutting off their Medicaid."

But Jefferson would advocate efforts to promote peace, harmony, and understanding between black and white Americans. Not focusing on past wrongs, but looking to a brighter future. Programs like affirmative action that produce white resentment over "reverse discrimination" and indulge black feelings of "victimhood" won't promote healthy race relations. Mutual respect and forbearance, with hope for the future, is the only way, Jefferson would believe, to break the cycle of bitterness and hatred.

The battleground over affirmative action (federal and state policies that encourage hiring and promoting people with equal qualifications from groups historically discriminated against, such as blacks and women) also reflects the underlying mistrust between the races in this country. When California voted by a 55 percent majority to end affirmative action in that state, a black federal judge issued a restraining order, preventing the law from being implemented, on the grounds that there was a "strong probability" that Proposition 209 was unconstitutional. Governor Pete Wilson, who made his national GOP career on attacking affirmative action, replied:

Proposition 209 prohibits discrimination against all races, and surely cannot be considered a violation of the Fourteenth Amendment, which was designed to prohibit all racial discrimination. The absurd consequences of this [federal] ruling is that California can constitutionally only prohibit discrimination against some races but cannot constitutionally prohibit discrimination against all races.

ACLU lawyer Mark Rosenbaum countered that the proposition was an attempt to "move white people to the front of the line."

Of the Nation of Islam, or Black Muslims, led by Louis Farrakhan, Jefferson would be disturbed. Any ethnic or cultural group that emphasized its "roots" outside America to the exclusion of other groups in the United States was denying the transforming effect of unique American civilization. Of a Native American "Prophet" who advocated very similar exclusive programs, Jefferson wrote:

> [He] is more rogue than fool . . . his declared object was the reformation of his red brethren, and their return to their pristine manner of living. He pretended to be in constant communication with the Great Spirit; that He was instructed by Him to make known to the Indians that they were created by Him distinct from the whites . . . for different purposes . . . that they must return from all the ways of the whites to the habits and opinions of their forefathers . . .

Jefferson found this early retreat to "multiculturalism" ridiculous (and destructive to the Native Americans that followed it).

And so, in American race relations, charge and countercharge go back and forth, just as Jefferson predicted. His only hope for improved racial relations in America was that over time the old hostilities might lessen; but it would be a very long time.

Five

POLITICAL LEADERSHIP

"There is a natural aristocracy among men. The grounds of this are virtue and talents."

—THOMAS JEFFERSON, 1813

Thomas Jefferson's leadership style might be characterized as informal but dignified, democratic but professional. Today we would call it "humanistic" leadership—which guides and "facilitates" without being authoritarian. He was kind, efficient, and civilized as a leader. He showed respect and courtesy to his followers, or what he would refer to as his "colleagues." As president, party leader, head of a plantation and family, as friend and host, Jefferson displayed extraordinary leadership qualities. He was, as one biographer put it, "an executive beyond compare." But his success depended on a mature, competent group of followers. His informal, respectful style assumed equally orderly, talented, and self-controlled associates.

When working with people of like mind and temperament, Jefferson's leadership worked wonderfully smoothly; when confronted with more haughty or self-assertive personalities (like a British ambassador), it failed miserably. For most of his career, Jefferson was blessed with colleagues who shared his vision of informal, collegial relations. There were some notable exceptions, but overall, Thomas

Jefferson was the kind of boss most of us would like to have, the kind of leader America has prospered under.

Jefferson as President

As president, Thomas Jefferson treated his cabinet members as partners and friends, rather than as employees or subordinates. It was as though he said to James Madison, Albert Gallatin, and the others, "I call you friends, not servants." He respected and liked his colleagues, once saying, "If I had a universe to choose from, I could not change one of my associates to my better satisfaction." He did not lord it over them that he was their president and boss; his personality was democratic and gracious.

Jefferson led his administration not by his formal authority, but by the persuasiveness of his reasoning and the charm of his personality. He ran cabinet meetings as gatherings of friends, not bureaucratic committees. The only rules were those of open, honest discussion, fair play, and mutual respect. His cabinet usually arrived at decisions in unison: consensus ruled over pluralism. When differences could not be resolved through discussion, requiring a vote to be taken to decide the issue, Jefferson's vote counted only as one among the many. He did not "pull rank"; he did not threaten or bully or intimidate or manipulate others. He respected their free will and judgment. Consequently, Jefferson's administration was marked by a harmony and loyalty that had been absent in Washington's and Adams's presidential administrations. President Jefferson, because of his democratic leadership style, "commanded" only the loyalty and respect of his associates. He was thus an "executive beyond compare," as one biographer put it.

As a leader, Jefferson combined formality and informality in a rarely effective way. There was no doubt he had authority, that he was in charge. But he wore the mantle of authority lightly, without presumption, pride, or arrogance. He was friendly and kind, without losing his commanding presence and dignity. It was a pleasure to work with him.

Of course, this democratic leadership style required a certain character of "follower." Independent, responsible, competent, Jefferson chose colleagues who were equal to him intellectually, morally, and circumstantially. James Madison is a good example of this: a leader in his own right ("Father of the Constitution"), self-motivated, professional, and dedicated. Madison was not intimidated by Jefferson. He disagreed with him often, frequently changing the president's mind by his persuasive reasoning. Jefferson did not want a group of toadies or lickspittles for followers. He abhorred yes-men and intellectual weaklings; he didn't want inferior disciples, but equal colleagues. Jefferson knew that hiring mediocre employees who would just worship and obey him would produce mediocre policy and worse. Small minds and petty hearts would breed infighting and intrigue. "Ill-defined limits of their respective departments, jealousies, trifling at first, but nourished and strengthened by repetition of occasions, intrigue without doors of designing persons to build an importance to themselves on the division of others, might from small beginnings, have produced persevering oppositions," he wrote.

President Jefferson's leadership qualities and his cabinet members' talents and loyalty produced a uniquely harmonious, happy organization, sharply contrasted with the administrations of Washington and Adams, where Federalists and Republicans, Hamiltonians and Jeffersonians, fought like cats and dogs. The embarrassments of internal dissensions, leaks, infighting, and bitterness were absent from Jefferson's administration. Differences of opinion naturally occurred, but Jefferson channeled them into constructive discussion and compromise by his example of openness, fair play, humility, and respect. He was never known to lose his temper, but conducted all business, as a biographer noted, with "politeness and grace." One is reminded of the recent administration of President George Bush, who treated his colleagues with respect and camaraderie—always gracious, often sending encouraging or congratulatory telephone calls or notes. President Clinton's administration has been rather different, as we will see later.

President Jefferson displayed a similar democratic leadership style in his relations with ordinary citizens. He took daily horseback rides around the new city of Washington, where he would meet and talk with tradesmen and farmers, women and men. On one such ride, he fell into conversation with a stranger who, not knowing whom he was talking to, mercilessly criticized the president of the United States. (Before the age of television and newspaper photographs, many did not know what the president looked like!) Mr. Jefferson calmly listened as the man cruelly mischaracterized and maligned him, then promised to introduce the stranger to that horrible President Jefferson the very next day!

The following day, Jefferson rode up to the man and introduced himself. The citizen was horrified to learn he'd criticized the president to his face, and apologized profusely. Jefferson laughed it off and put the man at ease by saying it was all right: the villain he'd described bore no resemblance to the real president.

Jefferson's political opponents ridiculed this practice of visiting the people daily as populist ostentation: a mere show of interest in "the masses"; demagoguery. The Federalists also ridiculed Jefferson's habit of opening the White House twice a year to the public—on July 4 and New Year's Day. These simple open houses, where citizens streamed through the White House to sample punch and cake and be greeted by the president, replaced the formal weekly levees of previous presidents, where the chief executive would sit on his throne like a king or pope and hold "audiences" with the few honored to be received. Jefferson found these levees pompous and ridiculous—dangerous imitations of what he called British "birthdays, levees, processions to Parliament, inauguration pomposities, etc." He similarly avoided the Washington, D.C., social life of parties, receptions, and theater as vain and foolish. Jefferson's White House was open and informal. "What a contrast," exclaimed a visitor who had experienced previous Federalist administrations: "Coteries and drawing rooms are no more; the promenade of superciliousness and dissipation no longer excites disgust . . ."

President Jefferson established a social style he thought appropriate to a young republic. During the morning hours he kept his office door ajar for callers both official and unofficial.

The most famous of his democratic social practices were Jefferson's White House dinners for congressmen and visiting dignitaries. In the young capital city of Washington, with few eating establishments or gracious homes, Jefferson's ample dinner table and wine cellar became a welcome respite from dull Washington dining life. He entertained congressmen loyal to his Democratic-Republican Party and members of the Federalist opposition. "I cultivate personal intercourse with the members of the legislature," he said, "that we may know one another and have opportunity of little explanations of circumstances, which, not understood, might produce jealousies and suspicions injurious to the public interest." His opponents cynically claimed he was wining and dining legislators to manipulate and control them. And it is true that after a tasty meal at the president's table, lubricated with plenty of French wine, Congress did seem to cooperate more with the Jefferson administration. His lively, charming conversation also won him many friends in other branches of the government.

Jefferson's dining room social life became an integral part of his political leadership, but that was common practice among Virginia gentlemen, where formal politics and informal society often mixed. Elegant surroundings and friendly conversation were a way of life in the Virginia gentry class.

At these White House dinners, formal rank and distinctions were ignored. As in his cabinet meetings, all guests were considered equal. The regal rectangular dinner table was replaced with a "republican" oval table, and seating was not designated—guests sat where they wished. Green canvas, instead of fancy rugs, covered the floor. Good French and American cuisine was served, in abundance. Servants were rarely on display. Jefferson led the conversation himself, hosting eight to ten guests, and often tactfully drawing into the talk the more retiring or shy persons around the table. He actually avoided political topics, since they might lead to unpleasant differences, relying on more neutral subjects of weather, agriculture, art, music, or literature. "Good humor and politeness never introduce into mixed society a question on which they foresee there will be a difference of opinion," he quipped. One guest found dinner at the president's house "an elegant mental treat."

Witty and smart, Jefferson always impressed his visitors—even those from the opposite party. John Quincy Adams, an ardent enemy of Jefferson's, nevertheless remarked after an evening's visit, "You never can be an hour in this man's company without something of the marvelous." Another political foe observed, "No one can know Mr. Jefferson and be his personal enemy."

Of course, there were a few exceptions. The most glaring was the famous case of the visiting British ambassador, a fellow ironically named Merry.

Minister Merry was accustomed to more dignity in his station—the formalities of Royal Court, the great respect and kowtowing of people to His Majesty's foreign service (like Sir Joseph Bilge in Gilbert and Sullivan's *H.M.S. Pinafore*). With Jefferson and his republican ways, Mr. Merry had a rude surprise.

The British minister arrived at the White House expecting a grand, ceremonious welcome. Instead, he found the reception room empty. Proceeding down the hallway to the president's study, he suddenly bumped into Jefferson wearing his slippers and casual clothes. Ambassador Merry fumed to his government, "I, in my official costume, found myself at the hour of reception . . . introduced to a man as President of the United States, not merely in undress, but *actually standing in slippers down at the heels,* and both pantaloons, coat, and under-clothes indicative of utter slovenliness and indifference to appearances, and in a state of negligence actually studied."

Mr. Merry concluded that this was a deliberate insult to his nation. And maybe it was. Maybe Jefferson decided to return the rudeness he had experienced when introduced at the British Court (where King George III turned his back on him). But probably not, for Jefferson always subscribed to the Christian principle: "Never return evil for evil." Instead, Jefferson was probably just absorbed in the work that morning, intellectually absorbed to the point of losing track of the time, dressed in his usual work attire (comfortable, casual clothes) that he wore to greet all alike: rich or poor, high or low, famous or obscure. But this republican manner infuriated the British ambassador. Coming from a government where the least lapse of etiquette caused offense and often international incidents, where big egos and wounded pride made life a continual series of haughty contempt and humiliating encounters, Minister Merry felt outraged at President Jefferson's appearance and treatment of him. He stormed out of the White House at this affront to his dignity.

Only by the cajoling of the secretary of state, James Madison, did the British ambassador agree to return to the White House, for a dinner a few nights later. There he faced further offense! Assuming the dinner was in his honor, Merry was outraged to find Louis Pichon, the French chargé d'affaires, also at the dinner (the English were at war with France at this time). Then President Jefferson escorted the attractive Dolley Madison into the dining room instead of following the proper protocol of taking Mrs. Merry's arm. (Mrs. Merry was a fat, old woman given to wearing gaudy jewels and dresses and sharing the haughty, boring manner of her husband.) Again, Minister Merry took this as a deliberate affront to himself and the British Crown. He fumed later to his government over the insulting behavior of the American president. Actually, Jefferson was merely practicing his usual style of entertaining: informal, unpretentious, casual. He probably just found Dolley Madison more pleasant company than Mrs. Merry and saw no reason to put himself through a tedious, boring ordeal. He probably laughed it off when Madison told him that Merry was enraged.

Thereafter, the British ambassador refused to have social contact with Jefferson. When invited to meet or dine at the White House, the minister refused, saying he'd have to ask his government for instructions. Secretary of State Madison was astonished by this conduct, saying that it was a "display of diplomatic superstition truly extraordinary in this age and in this country." President Jefferson also couldn't believe it. "We have told [Merry] that the principle of society as well as of government with us is the equality of individuals composing it; that no man here would come to a dinner where he was to be marked with inferiority to any other." To Merry's insistence that he consult his government before attending any more meals, President Jefferson mocked him to Madison, saying, "I shall be highly honored when the King of England is good enough to let Mr. Merry come and eat my soup."

As party leader, Jefferson showed the same informal, respectful style of leadership. A mobilizer and organizer of the anti–Federalist Party called the Democratic-Republican Party, Jefferson assisted development of local party units, party newspapers, party pamphleteers and correspondence. He encouraged greater party discipline in Congress but didn't try to "micromanage" the state and local party organizations. While serving as vice president under John Adams, he helped develop the nascent Democratic-Republican Party, using similar tactics employed later as president. He lodged at Francis' Hotel, and during dinners with congressional lodgers he talked politics and philosophy, shaping party strategy and policy. President Adams and other Federalists began to resent Jefferson's mixing of formal and informal party activity. This wasn't helped when a letter of T. J.'s was leaked to the press in which he lambasted the Federalists as "the apostates who have gone to these heresies, men who were Sampsons in the field and Solomons in the council, but who have had their heads shorn by the harlot England."

Jefferson believed that American democracy required quality leadership. And quality leadership is not possible without quality citizenship. That's why (at the state and local levels) Jefferson wanted extensive public services—in public education, welfare, and political activity—to cultivate an intelligent citizenry and prepare good leaders for the nation. Such social programs, for Jefferson, were to provide opportunities for every condition, "without regard to wealth, birth, or other accidental condition," to be "fitly formed and disposed to become useful instruments for the public."

Those national leaders would be admirable, for Jefferson, if they were virtuous and talented, wise and good: a "natural aristocracy." Leaders who had not entered government for the prestige, the money, the fame, or the power, but for service—out of love of country, gratitude to America. This Jeffersonian natural aristocracy was composed of those individuals distinguished by their "genius and virtue" or "wisdom and goodness" for genuine leadership. "The natural aristocracy I consider," Jefferson said, "the most precious gift of nature for the instruction, the trusts, and the government of society."

Jefferson distinguished this virtuous aristocracy (which could be born in any class of people) from what he called the pseudo-aristocracy of wealth or birth (family). The rich and famous were a "tinsel aristocracy" without necessarily either virtue or talents. Your name may be Rockefeller or Roosevelt or Kennedy, but that didn't guarantee your character, intelligence, or sense of public duty, for Jefferson. This pseudo-aristocracy of money or family connections was more likely to be "a mischievous ingredient in government," according to Jefferson. Hence, he disliked European hereditary aristocracy and monarchy ("transmitted through the loins of knaves and fools, passing from the debauches of the table to those of the bed") and the newly rich of the Hamiltonian Federalists: bankers, lawyers, stockbrokers, business tycoons (like Ross

Perot). Neither make good, public-spirited, wise rulers. Rather, they make corrupt, dishonest, self-absorbed, prideful, arrogant bozos, the very people the Federalist John Adams admired when he said, "who are the [aristocrats]? . . . the World, Mankind, have by their practice always answered 'The rich, the beautiful and well born.' " For Jefferson, these spelled doom for the American democracy.

How do contemporary leaders measure up to Jefferson's standards of leadership? Bill Clinton's humble beginnings leading to Georgetown University, Oxford, Yale, and political prominence through intelligence and hard work seem to satisfy Jefferson's qualifications for a natural aristocrat. Yet Clinton's lack of principle, frequent moral lapses, need for prominence, and general untrustworthiness cast a shadow over his Jeffersonian leadership qualities. The recent book by Bob Woodward on the Clinton administration, *The Agenda,* shows anything but the civilized, respectful leadership style of Jefferson. Instead of rational discussion, mutual respect, and arriving at decisions by consensus, one reviewer finds Woodward's exposé of the Clinton administration revealing "the fights, the backbiting, the bitch-fests, the recriminations, the pep-talks, the maneuvering . . . detailed here, page after vicious . . . page."

Unlike Jefferson's calm, rational leadership, President Clinton lapses into fits of anger, verbally abusing his colleagues as his violent stepfather physically abused his mother. When once learning of a scheduling mistake, Clinton flew into a fit of rage, screaming: "Who the hell could make such a dumb fucking mistake?" Clinton's close adviser Dick Morris told the prostitute he frequented that Clinton's nickname was "the Monster" for his frequent fits of rage.

At other times, Woodward shows, Clinton could be charming and ingratiating, especially with outside constituencies (Hollywood personalities, gay leaders, women's groups, White House interns); but his principles seem to change with the audience he addresses. His close associate George Stephanopoulos described Clinton as "a kaleidoscope," changing attitudes depending on his environment.

Journalist Joe Klein described Clinton's character and leadership style as "promiscuous." Spilling over from his sexual promiscuity, Clinton, according to Klein, is best understood as "indiscriminate" in his attachment to policies and principles, the classic politician trying to come down on all sides of all issues (what opponents in his presidential elections called waffling). Former President Bush said Clinton would turn the White House into "the Waffle House." Maybe that's better than some presidents trying to turn it into a whorehouse, but Clinton's rapid changes in policy on Haiti, gays in the military, Bosnia, and welfare both frustrate his opponents with a moving target and belie the principled consistency of President Jefferson.

Foreign leaders mistrust Clinton. Increasing scandals present a troubling image of the sleazy, "poor white southern trash" background of an Arkansas "Slick Willie." Untrustworthy. A fraud. Dishonest. Disingenuous. Claiming to have grown up in "a little town called Hope" but actually reared in the southern gangster city of Hot Springs, Arkansas. A background and style hardly resembling Jefferson's. And yet Bill Clinton has the intelligence, determination, and energy characteristic of Jefferson's natural aristocrat. "The Comeback Kid," if he finds some principles and moral strength, may yet, in his second term as president, surprise us all, and end up deserving the "Jeffersonian" title that he so covets. Or his moral lapses may bring down his presidency.

Even before that, however, Clinton's reelection as president tells us more about the American citizenry than about its leader. Jefferson's natural aristocracy required a disciplined, moral citizenry to elect it. What does it say about American culture that a majority of people will tolerate moral laxity, dishonesty, and lack of principles so long as its leadership seems sympathetic to the common person's problems and empathetic to its desires?

Supporters of Republican Newt Gingrich soon found their hero less than perfect also. The House Subcommittee on Ethics fined Newt $300,000 and reprimanded him for using contributions to his tax-exempt foundation to finance a college course that aimed to get GOP candidates elected. The report concluded that "the violation does not represent only a single instance of reckless conduct. Rather, over a number of years and in a number of situations, Mr. Gingrich showed a disregard and lack of respect for the standards of conduct that applied to his activities."

Jefferson had in mind a person of *noblesse oblige,* one who not merely wants to serve in order to bring glory to himself but is devoted to the nation, a person unconcerned about attacks on himself so long as he knows he is serving his country. That's why Jefferson regarded his own presidency as a "burden" and a "splendid misery." It was not fun for him. He could have had more fun staying at Monticello, riding a horse or inventing a new clock. But it was a privilege to sacrifice his own comfort and ease to be serving the United States.

Surprisingly, Jefferson would see a Republican, President George Bush, as embodying those ideals. Bush could have been more happy, have more ease and pleasure, playing golf. He could have made more money staying in business. He entered politics to serve the country that had blessed him and his family. Barbara Bush's autobiography exhibits this quality.

Jefferson would also admire President Ronald Reagan as he admired George Washington: "possessing neither copiousness of ideas, nor fluency of words . . . He was, indeed, in every sense of the words, a wise, a good, and a great man."

Jefferson would see President Jimmy Carter the way he would see Bush. That Carter entered politics out of moral motives has been confirmed by the diplomatic and charitable activities he has undertaken since his retirement as president. Carter has developed several new careers (writer, poet, housebuilder, and peacemaker), not unlike Jefferson's post-presidential stints as writer, negotiator, architect, and founder of a university. Carter is best known for his international peace efforts—personally negotiating agreements (and preventing wars) in Haiti, Korea, and Sudan. He deals with the "untouchable" dictators in the world and wins their confidence. Carter succeeds where others fail because, he says, "I'm a patient listener." He shows respect to those whom the world regards as brutal monsters—and averts bloody military campaigns. He seems to be effective, as he was earlier in the Israeli-Egyptian peace accords, by actually living the Christian precept of "loving the sinners" while hating the sin that destroys them. His attachment to principle, like Jefferson's, gives him a strength (and freedom from what other people think of him) that is just the opposite of Clinton's "promiscuity." Carter's lasting legacy is the Carter Center—a 100,000-square-foot office complex on a thirty-five-acre site two miles from downtown Atlanta, Georgia. Most of the Center's 250 employees (and 100 student interns) live in the Atlanta area, but field representatives reside in Guyana, Liberia, Ethiopia, Nicaragua, and other international locations. With an annual budget of $26 million, the Carter Center focuses on promoting political democracy, economic development, health care, and urban rejuvenation around the world. It encompasses thirteen main programs serving over thirty nations with the principle of improving life for "the least among us" as its underlying purpose. Adjacent to the Jimmy Carter Library, it has conference facilities and is known as one of the most effective nonsectarian, nongovernmental organizations of international relief in the world. Like Jefferson's University of Virginia, Jimmy Carter's center embodies the values he personally held dear and will affect humanity long after he has gone to his reward. Among its chief programs are the African Governance Program; the Commission on Radio and Television Policy; the Global Development Initiative; the Human Rights Program; Latin American and Caribbean Program; an Environmental Initiative; Interfaith Health Program; Tobacco Control Program; Task Force on Child Survival; and Anti–River Blindness Program. In all of these, Carter uses the contacts he made as president to solve serious world problems. When skeptics criticize him for being overly optimistic, he recounts the story of the boy who throws beached starfish back into the sea.

When a cynic laughs that he can't save them all, the boy replies, "But I can save this one and it sure makes a difference to him!" For example, the democratic procedures that Americans take for granted (such as voting in secret ballots) are unknown in several sub-Saharan African countries. In 1991 Carter led an international observer team to monitor voting fairness in Zambia's first free election. In 1992 the Carter Center Team monitored Ghana's first democratic presidential election in over thirty years. In Liberia the center provided assistance on democratic voting procedures after years of bloody civil war in that country. With Mikhail Gorbachev, the Carter Center provided advice to the newly liberated media in the former Soviet countries through a Commission on Radio and Television Policy. The idea of free, fair news coverage was an unknown concept in Russia, and the Carter Center's initiative helped five hundred radio and television stations in the former Soviet Union learn western notions of journalistic freedom and responsibility. In 1986 Carter and a philanthropist established the Carter-Menil Human Rights Prize, giving $100,000 to individuals and oranizations that advance human rights to adequate food, shelter, medical services, and safety. One winnner of the prize was the Haitian Refugee Center of Miami. The center's Human Rights Program has also provided training to police forces in Guyana and Ethiopia. Typically, the Center's emphasis is on groups being persecuted for their religious beliefs or political ideals. In South America the twenty-five-member Council of Freely Elected Heads of Government is headquartered in the center's Latin American and Caribbean Program. This advances democratic practices in those countries and resolves conflicts among the countries in the region. Encouraging agricultural productivity in the third world has led to increases in grain production (in Sudan 500 percent more wheat during 1991–92 than 1986–87; in Ghana, 143 percent more corn from 1985 to 1993) with support from the Carter Center. The center's Interfaith Health Program encourages Christians, Muslims, and Jews to cooperate in providing health care to the needy in their communities. Visiting the sick and elderly, educating children on the risks of drugs and guns, and providing immunizations to poor children have been initiated under this program. The Carter Center's Tobacco Control Program advocates higher taxes on this deadly drug and providing education to young people on its effects on their health. Working with sponsors UNICEF, the Rockefeller Foundation, the World Bank, and others, Carter's Task Force on Child Survival successfully raised the immunization rate of the world's young from 20 percent to 80 percent in six years. The Carter Center got the pharmaceutical company Merck to donate medicine to control river blindness—a disease that affects 18 million people in Africa and Latin America.

The phenomenal influence of the Carter Center grew out of the former president's realization that power continues after leaving the White House: "When we came home from the White House, we realized we still had vast resources. I mean anybody will help you with anything because you were President. All you have to do is ask them . . . it was important to us to help those less fortunate . . . it developed into something we never dreamed it would be."

Jefferson would hope for natural aristocrats to lead America in the future. Why are more natural aristocrats (of virtue and talents) not going into politics in contemporary America? Because public life has become much worse than the "splendid misery" that Jefferson experienced. The ruthless harassment of public candidates and officials by the press, the loss of any real authority to function effectively, and the negative image of politicians have persuaded the most gifted people in the United States that they can be happier and more effective in corporate, academic, or professional careers. This leaves the political field to the ambitious, sleazy, and arrogant. Only a more responsible, self-restrained media and more respectful populace will make service in the public realm attractive again to the most decent and gifted.

Personal Leadership

Jefferson's style of leadership extended to his personal domain, showing that he didn't compartmentalize his life into public and private, but displayed the same character in both. As head of a large family and plantation, member of a vast community of friends, and host to innumerable guests, Jefferson conveyed a distinctive mode of leadership.

As a father of two daughters, he was a strict but affectionate patriarch. In a letter to Patsy, Jefferson prescribed to the girl a daily regimen almost military in rigor: "From 8 to 10 o'clock practice music. From 10 to 1 dance one day and draw another. From 1 to 2 draw on the dance day and write a letter the next day. From 3 to 4 read French. From 4 to 5 exercise yourself in music. From 5 till bedtime read English, write, etc." Apparently young girls didn't eat meals in the eighteenth century! He also admonished his daughters on their dress and habits: "I do not wish you to be gayly clothed at this time of life, but that what you wear should be fine of its kind; but above all things, and at all times let your clothes be clean, whole, and properly put on . . . Nothing is so disgusting to our sex as a want of cleanliness and delicacy in yours."

While a demanding father, he was also an affectionate one, frequently writing to his daughters how much he loved them. His children returned that parental love, touchingly beginning letters to "My dear Papa." As in his political life, Jefferson ruled with a light touch. A granddaughter recalled, "I never heard him utter a harsh word to one of us, or speak in a raised tone of voice, or use a threat." He taught the children games, lavished gifts on them, included them in his walks around Monticello, where "his cheerfulness and affection were the warm sun in which his family all basked and were invigorated." Like his associates in government, Jefferson's kin responded to his skillful and kind leadership with loyalty and affection. A visitor to his home wrote that "it was delightful to observe the devoted and respectful attention that was paid him by all the family."

Thomas Jefferson ruled his servants (he would never have called them his "slaves") with similar deference and mildness. His personal boyhood slave, Jupiter, was more like a brother than a servant. The master's conviction that slavery was a terrible moral evil led him to try and mitigate its worse excesses. He would not allow slaves to be overworked or beaten. He managed them with material incentives rather than force, "on the comfortable footing of the laborers of other countries." He claimed that he "loved industry and abhorred severity." Martha Randolph remembered that the slaves at Monticello thought her father was "one of the greatest, and they knew him to be one of the best men and kindest of masters." An overseer on his plantation, Edmund Bacon, recalled that Jefferson "was always very kind and indulgent to his servants. He would not allow them to be at all overworked, and he would hardly ever allow one of them to be whipped . . . He could not bear to have a servant whipped, no odds how much he deserved it." The Monticello slaves returned the kindness of their master with extraordinary loyalty and affection. When Jefferson returned home one Christmas after an extended absence, the slaves greeted his carriage with exuberance. "They collected in crowds around it," a witness wrote, "and almost drew it up the mountain by hand . . . When the door of the carriage was opened, they received him in their arms and bore him to the house, crowding around and kissing his hands and feet . . ." The frequently discussed charge that he kept a black slave mistress (see chapter 13, "Women") has still not been proved or disproved conclusively.

To guests and strangers he was a consummate host and gentleman. As discussed later (in the chapter on manners), Jefferson governed his relations with everyone with the same ease and grace he displayed as president. In a large circle of friends, including James Madison and James Monroe, he was by far the most famous and gifted, but he never dominated them, or even much younger men; rather, he showed them respect, treating others as he would like to be treated by them. This was the secret of Jefferson's leadership style, and it was his model for good American leadership.

Six

FAMILY VALUES

"It is in the love of one's family only that heartfelt happiness is known."

—THOMAS JEFFERSON, 1801

Jefferson believed in traditional family values; he just didn't always live up to them. When living at his country home, Monticello, he led a conventional family life, typical of the Virginia gentry. While living in Paris, however, he lived a more unconventional lifestyle (but who doesn't in Paris?).

Jefferson's Family

While he was married, Jefferson was a loving, faithful, and devoted husband to his wife, Martha (nicknamed Patty), and a caring and indulgent father to his daughters. Throughout his life he loved children, once quoting the Bible that "happy is the man who hath his quiver full." A great-granddaughter wrote of Jefferson's "beautiful domestic character," especially the "warmth of his affections." Jefferson frequently expressed his love for his children and grandchildren; he invented and played games with them and indulged them with frequent surprises and gifts. His granddaughter Ellen once wrote: "My Bible came from him, my Shakespeare, my first writing table, my first Leghorn hat, my first silk dress . . . Our Grandfather seemed to read our hearts, to see our invisible wishes . . ."

When Jefferson's young wife lay sick and dying, he attended her continually for four months, reading poetry to her, whispering his affection to her, encouraging and comforting her. When Martha finally died (after giving birth to their sixth child), he fell into such a deep depression that his family feared suicide. His grief never left him. He never remarried. A rather different picture from that of Newt Gingrich marching into his first wife's hospital room (where she was recovering from cancer surgery) to tell her he wanted a divorce.

But for the rest of his life (and forty-four years of widowhood), Jefferson loved the presence of his children, grandchildren, friends, and guests at his home, Monticello. He once described it as "living like an antediluvian patriarch," an Old Testament Abraham, amid the busy activity of servants and guests, the running-about of children and dogs, the flurry of many people. Often, when he would take a walk in the garden, he would call the children to join him, and a granddaughter remembers that "we raced after and before him and we were made perfectly happy by this permission to accompany him." At other times, Jefferson would retire to his study to read or write correspondence and leave strict instructions not to be disturbed. But often, he would read books in the family circle, the children following his example. "I have seen him raise his eyes from his book," a granddaughter recalled, "and look round on the little circle of readers, and smile."

When president and living alone in Washington, Jefferson wrote his daughter Mary, "I employ my leisure moments in repassing often in my mind our happy domestic society when together at Monticello, and looking forward to renewal of it. No other society gives me now any satisfaction, as no other is founded in sincere affection."

Unlike many fathers, Thomas Jefferson *expressed* his love and affection to his daughters. He was not afraid to tell them how much he loved them. In a typical letter to his eldest daughter, Polly, he wrote, "I with pleasure take up my pen to express all my love to you . . ."

Jefferson would see the family as the most important social unit for the care and affection that humans need to share, and would agree with contemporary conservative concerns over the decline of the American family—through high divorce rates, single-parent families, child abuse and neglect. Jefferson would endorse the stand that a healthy, just society requires healthy, stable families.

On the volatile issue of abortion, Jefferson called it the murder of children ("saticide," Latin: killing the seed, or murder of the unborn) and "repugnant to nature" because it violates what he called the most "powerful affection of parental love." Jefferson discussed this in his revision of the code of Virginia in the 1770s. He notes in a section of the different forms of murder that in previous English law the concealment by the mother of the death of an illegitimate child is considered proof of murder. The legal reasoning was that the shame of bearing a bastard child was such "to induce the mother of such a child to murder it, in order to conceal her disgrace." But Jefferson opposed this reasoning, saying, "So many children die before, or soon after birth that to presume all those murdered who are found dead, is a presumption which will lead us oftener wrong than right . . ." Besides, Jefferson argued, "if shame be a powerful affection of the mind, is not parental love also? Is it not the strongest affection known? . . . should we not give some weight to presumptions from parental love, an affection at least as strong, in favor of life?"

To support Jefferson's view of the power of natural parental affection, he would have been familiar with the most famous story illustrating Solomon's wisdom. In the story (1 Kings 3:16–28), two women dispute over the same infant son, each claiming to be its mother. King Solomon devises a sure way to discover the true mother, appealing directly to that maternal affection that would rather lose the baby than have it killed. As the Bible (NIV) says:

> Then the king said: "Bring me a sword." So they brought a sword for the king. He then gave an order: "Cut the living child in two and give half to one and half to the other." The woman whose son was alive was filled with compassion for her son and said to the king, "Please, my lord, give her the living baby! Don't kill him!' But the other said, "Neither I nor you shall have him. Cut him in two!" Then the king gave his ruling: "Give the living baby to the first woman. Do not kill him; she is his mother."

The interesting and unique quality of Jefferson's argument against abortion (or saticide, Latin for the murder of the "seed"; the Hebrew word for "seed" denotes not only semen but the produce of that seed, offspring, as in "the seed of Abraham") is not that it arises from the familiar religious proscription against murder or the natural rights philosophy that says the fetus is a human possessing legal rights; but rather, that it is based in an "affections" or moral sense philosophy. Jefferson regards abortion as not only murder of the pre-born child but the most "repugnant" form of murder because it violates the mother's strongest natural affection—for her children. In that sense, abortion almost "kills" the women performing it as much as it does the baby aborted. So today he would likely have as much sympathy for the women having abortions as the children killed by abortions, and reserve his greatest wrath for those who misled women into believing that having an abortion would not adversely affect them.

The public debate over abortion in America has been called the most divisive (and violent) social issue since slavery (which finally tore the country in two during the Civil War). Jefferson's unique perspective on it contributes an important historical and philosophical insight that deserves consideration during the debate.

With conservatives, Thomas Jefferson would advocate laws strengthening the traditional family, yet he didn't always enjoy the reality of such a family. He grew up in a large one, with six sisters and two brothers, but he lost his father when he was only fourteen, and his mother never remarried. After his father's death, Jefferson became particularly attached to his older sister, Jane, who shared his intellectual and musical interests, but she died in her twenties, leaving Thomas desolate again. Of his own six children, only two lived past infancy; and through much of his adult life, only one daughter, Martha, survived. When he died, Martha and her ten children, who had been living with Jefferson at Monticello, were thrown out of this family home because of Jefferson's bankruptcy, and had two state legislatures (South Carolina and Louisiana) not voted to grant Jefferson's descendants $10,000, they would have been destitute.

So, on the contemporary family values debate, Jefferson would be well acquainted with the issues involved: he personally knew both the "ideal" nuclear family and the loss of that ideal through tragedy and death.

The Current Family Values Debate

Much of the current debate in America over family values centers around the definition of "the family." Conservatives hold to the traditional Judeo-Christian view of the family as a mother and father (husband and wife) with their offspring (children) and possibly other relatives (grandparents, aunts, uncles, cousins, etc.) or adopted children. Conservatives believe this traditional form of the family ("a man will leave his father and mother and be united to his wife, and the two will become one flesh") is divinely ordained for specific purposes. Each family member has a role to play in the care, nurturance, and discipline of the others (the mother's affection, the father's discipline, and children mow the yard). Messing with this Godly form of family life has severe consequences for the individual and society, say conservatives (mental health, crime, juvenile delinquency, drug abuse, teen pregnancy, and suicide). Not that all nuclear families are as happy as Ozzie and Harriet (were they happy?) or the Cleavers of *Leave It to Beaver* (we know they weren't happy!), but just that it has a better chance of being a complete and healthy family than those "incomplete" families that start out with disadvantages. And conservatives admit that the ideal nuclear family has always been subject to loss and disruption through death, separation, infidelity, and disagreement over what flavor of ice cream to buy. Jefferson was certainly acquainted with the first three of these. But conservatives maintain that the biblical form of the family remains the model to which all should strive. They think there is such a thing as a "normal" family that's best for the individual and society.

Liberals find this definition of the family too restrictive. To them, a family is a set of relationships established by the people involved—*they* define their "family." It may be a couple consisting of one man and one woman. It may be a couple of two (homosexual) men; or two (lesbian) women. It might be (and, in America, frequently is) a single parent with children, or children raised by grandparents. It may include a dog, cat, or squirrel. Maybe the cat is married to the squirrel. Or a trisexual (male, female, and trees) man might have six "wives," three dogs, twelve kids, and a possum! Who's to say this isn't a family?! Who's to say it isn't "natural," so long as they love and respect each other (at least for the moment), according to liberals. To condemn such families by some outmoded religious prejudice—well, it's just discrimination! So say the liberals. Ask Donna Shalala.

Throughout his life, Jefferson experienced both the conservative, nuclear family (with wife, Martha, and the kids) and the liberal nonnuclear family (as a single parent raising two daughters and then as a grandfather helping raise his daughter's ten children after their father went mad). So Jefferson would agree with liberals that "those things can happen and we have to make the best of them."

But Jefferson would agree with conservatives that the traditional family is the ideal: that he would have preferred to have a father around as he grew up; that his daughters needed their mother as they grew up; that it would have been better for his grandchildren to have a loving father as well as a loving grandfather.

For Jefferson, the traditional family is a model to strive for and affirm. If it's dysfunctional, it should be fixed, not abandoned. Like the contemporary men's movement Promise Keepers, which extols men being loving and responsible to their wives and children, Jefferson would expect American men to behave themselves (at least most of the time!). The Million Man March to Washington, D.C., in 1995 saw African American men pledge to assume similar responsibility for the women and children in their lives.

Now, before and after his marriage, Jefferson didn't behave himself all that well. He tried to seduce a friend's wife (by naively—and unsuccessfully—slipping her romantic quotations from classical writers!). Later this episode became a "political liability" exploited by his political opponents (those starchy Federalists—the Pat Robertsons of the early 1800s), and Jefferson had to make a public apology to his friend. He wrote, "When young and single I offered love to a handsome lady. I acknowledge its incorrectness." Wow! Talk about a bold admission of guilt! It's almost as good as Clinton's "I feel her pain"! And Jefferson didn't even have to be sued in federal court before admitting it.

Jefferson in Paris

When Jefferson went to Paris, after his wife's death, he really cut loose. He became very "liberal" in his attitudes toward family values (though not as liberal as Ben Franklin, who spent much of his time in French brothels).

Although Jefferson criticized French society for its moral decadence, loose living, and "passions at sea without rudder or compass," he was soon sailing in the same direction. (His rudder seemed to be off course too!) He hung around libertine French salons, drinking in their sophistication with their wine. He flirted with another "handsome lady": Maria Cosway of Italian and English descent, beautiful and gifted in art and music. Her husband, a very short man who painted miniature portraits of the nobility, had many extramarital affairs, prompting Maria to retaliate. She "got even" with her unfaithful husband by flirting with a tall American.

Maria and Jefferson had a romantic picnic by themselves in the gardens of Château de Marly near Désert de Retz. Both often referred to this magical encounter in later letters. As a result, Jefferson wrote Maria his famous "Head and Heart" dialogue (which someone said "puzzled her then and misled romantics ever since"). It was a classic midlife crisis for Jefferson (he was forty-four years old). Elsewhere he wrote to Maria, "When Heaven has taken from us some object of our love [his wife, Martha], how sweet is it to have a bosom whereon to recline our heads [i.e., Maria], and into which we may pour torrents of our tears." (Maybe Thomas Jefferson should have stuck to political writing—like the Declaration of Independence.)

The affair, however, was not consummated; Jefferson was still mourning his wife's death. Despite the attractiveness of the temptation, he wrote, "When sins are dear to us, we are but too prone to slide into them again. The act of repentance itself is often sweetened with the thought that it clears our account for a repetition of the same sin . . ." Uh-oh. Jefferson was getting into deep water here!

In the end, Jefferson couldn't do it. He was still a loving, faithful husband, mourning the death of his young wife. As someone said, "Jefferson's primness limited his sophistication." He remained a virtuous American alien in a sinful European world. The "angelic" American woman was preferable to the "Amazon" women of the Old World, in his words.

He was probably glad to get back to the Puritan United States, where temptations for a handsome young widower were less intense. Still, even here, like another southern President, he probably "lusted in his heart" for Sally Hemings.

And most of all, he wished to be back among his family at Monticello. Jefferson wrote his daughter from Washington, of "the desire of being at home once more, and of exchanging labor, envy, and malice for ease, domestic occupation and domestic love."

Back at home in 1809, following two terms as president, he did just that. And he did so for the next seventeen years, until his death at age eighty-three. Home was where all his dreams led.

Jefferson at Home

A beautiful book of reminiscences of Jefferson's home life was compiled by his great-granddaughter Sarah Randolph. *The Domestic Life of Thomas Jefferson* contains innumerable remembrances of family and friends at Monticello. A granddaughter described "his cheerfulness and affection" as "the warm sun in which his family all basked . . ." His generosity was legendary. An eight-year-old granddaughter, Cornelia, saw another girl's beautiful silk dress and went up the stairs, crying, "I never had a silk dress in my life." The next day a package arrived from Charlottesville containing a silk dress for Cornelia. Another granddaughter remembered wanting handsome horseback riding equipment. "I was standing one bright day in the portico, when a man rode up with a beautiful lady's saddle and bridle . . . my heart bounded. These coveted articles were deposited at my feet. My grandfather came out of his room to tell me they were mine . . ."

Music was a common feature of Jefferson's home, with various family members playing different instruments and singing. His grandson recalled Mr. Jefferson playing the violin "and his grandchildren dancing around him."

On summer evenings he supervised races for the children. Jefferson would arrange the starting line—giving the smaller children the advantage of a few yards—and then drop a handkerchief to signal the start of the race around the house or lawn. This was probably the origin of the liberals' habit of comparing social and economic success to a race, and adjusting the starting line to benefit the weakest.

And the Jefferson home included the numerous houseguests that arrived in a constant stream during T. J.'s retirement. Another grandchild recalled that Monticello had

> persons from abroad, from all the States of the Union, from every part of the state, men, women and children . . . almost every day for at least eight months of the year, brought its contingent of guests. People of wealth, fashion, men in office, professional men, military and civil, lawyers, doctors, Protestant clergymen, Catholic priests, members of Congress, foreign ministers, missionaries, Indian agents, tourists, travellers, artists, strangers, friends . . . and very varied, amusing and agreeable was the society afforded by the influx of guests. I have listened to very remarkable conversations carried on round the table, the fireside, or in the summer drawing room . . .

He wrote personal letters to all his children and grandchildren, often enclosing a news story or poem "suited to their ages and tastes."

All was not always harmonious at the Jefferson home, however. Even Thomas Jefferson and his closest daughter, Martha, occasionally got on each other's nerves. She apparently didn't share his architectural enthusiasm for alcove beds and carried on a long emotional siege to have it turned into a more useful chamber. As she wrote: "I have at last succeeded in having my alcove turned into a closet . . . I laid regular siege to papa who bore it in dignified *silence* for some time, but I gave it to him for breakfast, dinner and supper, and breakfast again until he gave up in despair at last and when painted it will not disfigure the room at all . . ."

After his death, Jefferson's family found hidden in a drawer in his room little packages containing locks of hair of his wife, daughter, and infant children who had died. One, simply marked "Lucy," contained a beautiful golden curl.

Thomas Jefferson valued his family.

Seven

THE ECONOMY AND WELFARE

"If we can prevent the government from wasting the labors of the people, under the pretence of taking care of them, they must become happy."

—THOMAS JEFFERSON, 1802

Jefferson advocated a free market economy mixed with social help for the neediest. Jefferson enjoyed the personal economic life of one of Virginia's ruling gentry. He inherited more than five thousand acres of beautiful Virginia countryside from his father and acquired another six thousand acres through marriage. He owned almost two hundred slaves to work at least three plantations along with textile, nail, and other manufacturing plants. As an eighteenth-century country gentleman, he had to manage a complex and difficult economic organization. The benefits of his elevated station were obvious: a comfortable upbringing in a spacious country house, surrounded by beautiful open land in which to hunt, fish, and explore; a good education; exposure to a variety of commodities and products; an established and dignified place in society. Jefferson was economically privileged.

And Jefferson's personal economy was extensive. He loved to shop. He bought thousands of books that created a vast library (eventually forming the basis of the Library of Congress); he filled a cellar with fine imported and domestic wines; he owned an extensive wardrobe of clothes; he bought all manner of new inventions and products. Jefferson kept detailed accounts of his purchases, giving us a record of his personal economy. For example, on one shopping excursion in London, he bought: several books, a pair of boots, boot garter, chess sets, a copying press, gloves, a harness, a hat, maps, pistols, pocketbooks, scientific equipment, stockings, tools, toothbrushes, travel trunks, a walking stick, watch chains, tailor-made clothes, calico, shoes, slippers, and a harpsichord. This guy would feel right at home in a modern American shopping mall! Not surprisingly, he was in serious debt most of his life. When he retired as president, he was $10,000 in the hole; at his death he owed over $100,000.

The disadvantages of Jefferson's economic condition were also common to the Virginia gentry class: vagaries of agricultural markets, exorbitant debt to British bankers and merchants, and gradually exhausted soil—reducing productivity. These negative economic factors conspired to keep Jefferson on the edge of financial ruin most of his life, finally finishing him off with the Depression of 1819. All these realities affected his economic theories and outlook. But what most guided his thinking in economic matters was a hope for democratic America to be prosperous with fairly equal distribution of wealth throughout the country. In his draft constitution for Virginia in 1776, he included a provision for granting fifty acres to every citizen, recognizing that economic independence furthered political independence and honesty. He reformed the state laws of property rights and inheritance, allowing freer disposal of personal property and more equal distribution of inheritances. The old laws of primogeniture (which preserved large estates by restricting inheritance to the eldest son) and entail (which prohibited the division and sale of large landed estates) had the effect of insulating an established, concentrated wealthy class, which also reserved political power to itself. Jefferson's reforms broke the eastern Virginia oligarchy's control over economics and politics, requiring all to live under the discipline of a free market requiring talents and hard work. The old, established families of Tidewater Virginia saw him as an upstart.

He regarded private property as a right founded in nature, and American prosperity dependent on an economy balancing "agriculture, manufacture and commerce." Jefferson respected the wealth acquired through skill and industry and opposed radical schemes for taking from the rich to give to the poor: "To take from one, because it is thought his own industry and that of his fathers has acquired too much, in order to spare to others who, or whose fathers have not exercised equal industry or skill, is to violate arbitrarily the first principle of association: 'the *guarantee* to everyone a free exercise of his industry and the fruits acquired by it.' " The government should be frugal and efficient. He wrote, "We must push Congress to the uttermost in economizing." Go, Gingrich! Jefferson would appreciate the Republican Congress's moves to cut federal programs and reduce the national budget. "I am for a government rigorously frugal and simple, applying all the possible savings . . . to the discharge of the national debt," he wrote.

Yet, like Clinton and other Democrats, Jefferson would be for taxing the richest at a higher rate to support the neediest (widows, orphans, and the disabled). But for the able-bodied poor, Jefferson established a system of "workfare" in Virginia with his "Bill for the Support of the Poor." In it, provision is made for "setting the poor . . . to work" unless "lame, impotent, blind," or "not able to maintain themselves." (Impotent here means too weak or sick to work.) He would approve of the many new state welfare plans (including Virginia's, under Republican Governor Allen) that include able-bodied recipients of welfare performing public service work. Wisconsin's Work Not Welfare Program, Massachusetts's Department of Transitional Assistance, Utah's SPED (Single Parent Employment Demonstration Project), New Jersey's Family Development Program, and Virginia's Independence Program all employ Jefferson's policy of workfare. And best of all, they are designed by the *states,* not the federal government—adapted to the decentralized needs and opportunities of each region. Jefferson would be most pleased by this trend: taking the social welfare programs from the highly centralized and bureaucratic federal government and distributing them to the states, closer to the people; replacing welfare handouts that trap and dehumanize recipients with programs that reward work efforts and build self-esteem and good habits (like Colorado's Personal Responsibility and Employment Program). A valuable trend.

In Alabama, where the federal welfare maximum benefit for a family of three was $164 a month, the state recently required recipients to take any job they could get or lose their welfare. For example, in one rural county where the main employer is a catfish processing plant, welfare recipients were required to accept those minimum-wage jobs or be cut from welfare rolls. The work in the catfish factory is wet, cold, and smelly. One week, fourteen able-bodied welfare recipients were scheduled to begin work at the plant. Suddenly seven of them had found jobs elsewhere! The director of Alabama's program said, "Once you make it clear this is what's expected, then changes will occur. In that county, the word is out: you either find a job or you're going to work for the catfish plant."

In Wisconsin, where welfare benefits are dropped for people who refuse to work, the welfare rolls have been cut by 27 percent since 1987. This system required waivers from the federal government (as one state employee said, "going to Washington to kiss somebody's ring"). Jefferson would be saddened to see that such state initiatives still require "permission" from the federal bureaucracy.

California and New Jersey have cut welfare benefits to mothers who have babies while on welfare. The illegitimate births of welfare mothers then dropped 11.4 percent; but more abortions took place. Hence, conservatives face a dilemma: are babies' lives saved by continuing liberal welfare benefits, and does fiscal responsibility harm their moral agenda?

In Riverside County, California, job scouts were hired to place able-bodied welfare recipients in private employment; for every $1.00 invested by the government, $2.84 was saved from welfare budgets by finding jobs in the private sector for government dependents. Reformers believe that these changes will not only save public funds but encourage responsibility on the part of the poor. By the early 1990s nearly one-third of all American births were to unmarried mothers. The cost of this in public welfare, day care, health care, and crime is astronomical. So personal responsibility and family values have a direct impact on government policy and programs.

Critics of Jeffersonian workfare programs claim it is instituting a new form of slavery: to either low-paying private employment or enforced public service work. But even a British critic of such "punitive, compulsory workfare" admits that "most American workfare schemes, for all their differences, have been shown to have a beneficial effect on participants' self-esteem." Jefferson, as his 1770s plan shows, would agree on the efficacy of the new workfare programs and would be pleased that they are emanating from the *states,* where the best domestic policy will always come from. An old idea is new again.

Jefferson's goal for the American economy was a nation of self-sufficient persons, which would make for the most virtuous, independent citizens. He extolled farmers, whom he called "the chosen people of God," because their husbandry made them free and self-sufficient. And that leads to social peace and happiness. "Every one, by his property, or satisfactory situation, is interested in the support of law and order." For Jefferson, the government does have an interest in maintaining full employment and prosperity. Without them, democracy is threatened.

Early in his career, that meant an agrarian nation, an America of small yeoman farmers—no big cities, factories, merchants, or bankers. As he wrote, "Were I to indulge my own theory I should wish [us] to practice neither commerce nor navigation, but to stand with respect [to the world] precisely on the footing of China. We should thus avoid wars, and all our citizens would be husband-men." But soon he realized that a purely agricultural, nontrading America would be not only unrealistic in the complex economies of the world but dangerous, as aggressive nations attack the peace-ful, isolated, pastoral ones. "We must now place the manufacturer by the side of the agriculturalist . . . [Anyone] against domestic manufacture must be for reducing us either to dependence on that foreign nation or to be clothed in skins, and to live, like wild beasts, in dens . . . manufactures are now as necessary to our in-dependence as to our comfort." What would he think of American manufacturing moving ever increasingly abroad (Mexico, China, the Philippines) to cheap labor markets? At some point it could endanger our security if new American manufacturing didn't keep up with it.

Jefferson the farmer became an effective advocate and practi-tioner of domestic manufacturing and international commerce. He negotiated favorable trade agreements for American producers throughout the European continent. He wrote a treatise on the whaling industry to encourage France to purchase American whale oil, and built a Franco-American trading system to break Britain's monopoly on American commerce. Yet he always despised large cities, remarking that "New York, like London, seems to be a cloa-cina of all the human depravities of human nature."

Jefferson's economics evolved as he learned how the world worked. They developed into what became known as the American system: our agricultural surpluses brought in foreign capital; Amer-ican manufactures grew by free world trade and selective protective tariffs; economic prosperity allowed a government run on low taxes, able to build infrastructure (roads, canals, etc.) which support a vital private economy solely on revenues, not on federal debt. As he put it: "An equilibrium between the occupation of agriculture, manufactures and commerce shall simplify our foreign concerns to the exchange only of the surplus which we cannot consume for those articles of reasonable comfort or convenience which we cannot produce." A diversified, vast national economy, providing almost all we need domestically, an enormous market (which the world continually caters to), and equal economic opportunity rewarding talents and hard work realize Jefferson's economic dream for America.

Jefferson most often identified poverty with ignorance, laziness, and bad social policy. He was horrified by the "mobs of the cities" in Europe, whose "ignorance, poverty and vice" made them unfit for rule. He feared that if political power ever fell into the hands of the urban masses, policy would "be instantly perverted to the demolition of everything public and private." The anger and hatred of the oppressed made them a dangerous element in politics, as evidenced in the French Revolution. The solution is a system to make as many citizens economically self-sufficient, and therefore responsible, as possible. "Everyone, by his property," he wrote to John Adams, "or by his satisfactory situation [employment] is interested in the support of law and order. And such men may safely and advantageously reserve to themselves a wholesome control over their public affairs." After Aristotle, Jefferson held that an economically independent, confident citizenry was necessary for a virtuous, honest republic.

On international trade, Jefferson favored "free commerce with all nations," assuming they reciprocated. Where other countries (like Japan today) want to have American markets, but close their markets to us, Jefferson advocated stiff tariffs on foreign goods. "Where a nation imposes high duties on our productions or prohibits them altogether, it may be proper for us to do the same by theirs . . ." he wrote.

While president, Jefferson faced English and French prohibitions on American trade and responded by a total embargo on foreign goods. "Assailed in our essential rights by two of the most powerful nations on the globe, we have remonstrated, negotiated and . . . retired . . . in the hope of peaceably preserving our rights."

He knew the frustration of dealing with unscrupulous trading partners.

Trade tariffs were, for Jefferson, peaceful alternatives to trade wars. So he would applaud recent moves to respond strongly to Japanese, Chinese, and European unfair trade practices, such as taking the U.S. case against Japan to the World Trade Organization, accusing them of collusion in shutting out American competition in car and auto parts markets. Japan's trade and industry minister, Ryutaro Hashimoto, displayed characteristic arrogance when he replied to such threats with the remark: "If you Americans force IBM dealerships to sell Fujitsu computers," his country might open up its auto and auto parts markets to American goods. This Japanese minister compared his dealings with U.S. Trade Representative Mickey Kantor to the treatment he gets from his wife when he returns home late and drunk. In Japanese culture such a comparison is an enormously caustic insult to the American official.

Jefferson faced similar insults and distortions from French and British trade officials. His reply was to cut off imports from those countries. The Clinton administration's move to tack a 25 percent tariff on Japanese luxury cars (up from 2.5 percent), such as Toyota's Lexus, Honda's Acura Legend, and Nissan's Infiniti, reflects a Jeffersonian approach to international trade.

Unfortunately, the world economy is much more intertwined in the late twentieth century than it was in Jefferson's time. Many Lexus and Infiniti dealers are Americans who combine them with Cadillac and Lincoln dealerships. They are heavily leveraged with thin profit margins, and the loss of foreign car sales could ruin them. Most American auto manufacturers are in a few midwestern states like Michigan and Ohio, but Japanese dealerships are in all fifty states—exerting pressure on Congress from more representatives not to raise tariffs. So, in a way, Jefferson's trade embargo policy in the early 1800s was simpler to implement than it is today.

International economics are more complex, requiring a Harvard or UVA Darden School M.B.A. that Jefferson did not have. Still, his general prescriptions for a healthy, prosperous American economy are remarkably timely.

EDUCATION

*"If a nation expects to be ignorant and free . . . it ex-
pects what never was and never will be."*

—THOMAS JEFFERSON, 1816

Thomas Jefferson was educated privately, but he believed in public education in America. It is necessary to avoid tyranny,
strengthen democracy, and provide equal opportunity.

*"Enlighten the people generally and tyranny and oppressions of
body and mind will vanish like spirits at the dawn of day."*

Our system of education in America will have political, economic, and social consequences, according to Jefferson.

Jefferson himself received a private education, common to the
eighteenth-century Virginia gentry class. He studied with a tutor
(an Anglican clergyman), attended college at William and Mary,
and read the law under George Wythe. His education was strictly
classical: Latin, Greek, and modern languages; great literature
(Shakespeare, etc.); ancient philosophy (Greek and Roman); the
Judeo-Christian tradition; and science/mathematics ("natural philosophy"). From this classical education came Jefferson's depth of
thought and grace of prose. His advocacy of a public system of

education in Virginia did not diminish his love of traditional learning—instead he simply wanted to give the advantages of a classical education to *all,* "regardless of wealth, birth or other accidental condition."

Jefferson began his education at the age of five in a one-room plantation schoolhouse at the estate in central Virginia called Tuckahoe, on the James River. There, he and his sisters and cousins learned the basics of reading, writing, and arithmetic from a private tutor. At the age of nine, like a good upper-class English boy, Jefferson was sent off to board at a classical "prep" school run by an Anglican clergyman in Goochland County, Virginia, east of Charlottesville. Rev. William Douglas, from Scotland, taught young Jefferson the rudiments of Greek and Latin. Jefferson later remarked that "to read the Latin and Greek authors in their original is a sublime luxury," and he added, "I thank on my knees him who directed my early education for having put into my possession this rich source of delight . . ." He also began to learn French, which he later read and spoke fluently.

At age twelve Thomas moved to the parish school of another Anglican divine, Rev. James Maury, "a correct classical scholar." Now he studied the ancient languages in depth, along with the Bible, English literature, history, geography, and mathematics. His master possessed a library of four hundred volumes, giving young Jefferson his first taste of the universe of learning.

Jefferson would later remember these school days as among the happiest of his life, shared with other boarding boys. And their student lives were not all work with no play. Like all country boys in Virginia, they went hunting in the mountain woods for deer, fox, turkey, partridge—and at night for raccoon and possum. And Jefferson would never shoot a hare or other game animal "settin'," but would always "scare em up" to give them a sporting chance. He loved walking and riding outdoors in the beautiful fields and forest of Virginia. Nature was an early teacher of Jefferson. Its wild but glorious ways always made him long for his mountains and contemplation.

Yet, despite his love of outdoor activities with boyhood companions, Jefferson at this youthful stage was already a diligent, self-disciplined student. One of his classmates at Maury's school said that he would "withdraw from the noisy crowd of his schoolfellows, learn the next day's lesson," and then rejoin them in their revelries. Late in life, Jefferson recalled that he was always "a hard student . . . and now, retired and at the age of seventy-six, I am again a hard student." His family remembers Jefferson studying fifteen hours a day while at college.

That college was William and Mary, in Williamsburg, Virginia, where Jefferson started at age sixteen. It was a common college for Virginia gentry boys to attend, those who didn't return to England for their education at Oxford or Cambridge or retreat to "Yankee" schools like Princeton (as friend James Madison did) or Harvard. Jefferson found William and Mary College disappointing architecturally: "rude, misshapen piles, which, but that they have roofs, would be taken for brick-kilns." This may account for his designing the architectural masterpiece of "the Lawn" when he founded the University of Virginia fifty years later.

The college Jefferson attended was a strange hodgepodge of schools: a divinity school for training Anglican ministers, a prep school, an Indian school for Christianizing the Native Americans, and a philosophy (or liberal arts) school, which Jefferson attended. About one hundred students were served by seven professors. The president of William and Mary was a notorious drunkard. Jefferson studied logic, physics, "ethicks," and mathematics. He was fortunate to study under a new professor, William Small, "a man profound in most of the useful branches of science, with a happy talent of communication, correct and gentlemanly manners, and an enlarged and liberal mind." Dr. Small tutored Jefferson in math, science, logic, ethics, rhetoric, and literature. He was a remarkable scholar, teacher, and companion, providing Jefferson with the role model of the intellectual, civilized Renaissance man that T. J. was to be known for. He was a sterling conversationalist from whom the rustic boy from Albemarle County learned the breadth and sophistication of the old country. When Small returned to England a few years later, he was an active member of the illustrious society of James Watt, Erasmus Darwin, and others of British science and technology. At Williamsburg he gave Jefferson his soon-to-be-famous graceful style of prose, reasoned thought, and carefully framed arguments (as in the Declaration of Independence).

More important, perhaps, Professor Small introduced young Jefferson to the elevated social life of Williamsburg (which Tom had referred to as "Devil's-Burg" previously, for its vulgar, wanton dissipations). Dr. Small frequently dined at the royal governor's mansion with leaders of Virginia politics, especially the brilliant lawyer George Wythe. Jefferson soon tasted of the governor's dinners and elegant, witty, urbane society. It was an exceptional part of his education, where, he later wrote, he "heard more good sense, more rational and philosophic conversations than all my life besides. They were truly Attic societies." The governor's "taste, refinement and erudition" Jefferson imitated later in life (see chapter 5, "Political Leadership") when he was president of the United States and hosted dinners at the White House for senators and congressmen. This Williamsburg of ruling society was, as one biographer put it, "Jefferson's university." He once called it "the finest school of manners and morals that ever existed in America."

Meeting lawyer-scholar Wythe probably led Jefferson to go on to read the law. After a brief apprenticeship in his mentor's law office, Jefferson was set loose, like a modern graduate student, with an extensive reading list and time to gather his thoughts. His self-discipline in study made such independent research possible and profitable. Besides the classic text on Anglo common law, the seventeenth-century *Institutes of the Laws of England*, by Sir Edward Coke (whom even scholar Jefferson considered an "old dull scoundrel"), he read philosophy (Bolingbroke), political theory (Aristotle, Locke), literature (Shakespeare), and religion (Milton).

Law was to be studied with its historical, philosophical, theological, and literary foundations, for Jefferson. This is what made him the "great synthesizer" of the American Revolution—using not just dry legal terminology in the cause of independence and democracy but literary allusions, historical examples, philosophical arguments, theological justifications. The classics of the past to illuminate the future. The keen logic of the ancients to guide the feet of the modern world. For Jefferson, traditional learning was not a dead, boring series of names and dates, but vital principles that critique and shape the future. Stimulating truths that spark a seeking mind and soul. Essential principles, whether in ancient Saxon liberties, Greek politics, or the Sermon on the Mount. To be applied to the present in a lively, vibrant spirit.

Soon after completing his own legal training, Jefferson was asked by a younger man to mentor him. He gave the new law student a rigorous regimen of study displaying his catholic approach. Throughout, he recommended "commonplacing" one's studies: writing out, in a separate notebook or journal, the quotes from authors the student found most interesting. Jefferson himself had done this as a law student, providing us with valuable insights into his studies and learning. He occasionally wrote his own comments on the excerpted materials, which give us a view into his thinking at the time. First, a grounding in Latin, French, mathematics, natural history, and philosophy. Then a daily regimen of athletic proportions. From dawn to 8:00 A.M., study the physical sciences, ethics, and religion. From eight to noon, the best hours of the day, study "the black-letter of the law"—classic texts (Magna Carta, English statutes, Bracton, Lord Kames, Sir Edward Coke, etc.). From noon to one o'clock, read politics (Locke, Sidney); in the afternoon, ancient and modern history; in the evening, literature, literary criticism, rhetoric, and oratory. Jefferson evidently didn't prescribe time for meals (law students probably couldn't afford them anyway) or remedies for eyestrain. Students at the University of Virginia might be grateful he went into public service instead of an academic career!

In the contemporary "traditional education" versus "multiculturalism" debate, Jefferson would side with the traditionalists. He would recommend American schools teach the basics and the classics: the time-honored works of Greek and Roman civilization, the Judeo-Christian tradition, good English literature, and classical languages. Ironically, from Jefferson's life experience, this classical education gave him the background to be one of the great revolutionaries in history and an advocate of social and scientific progress. A classical curriculum for American schools (along with traditional discipline) will not, for Jefferson, make us backward or reactionary, or retard our progressive tendencies.

"Multiculturalism" in American education argues that our country is not a single culture or a "melting pot" in which all immigrants give a distinctive flavor, but a mixture of distinct, separate cultures (African Americans, Hispanic, Asian, lesbian, etc.) that deserve to be kept distinct and affirmed, along with the dominant white, European, Christian culture that originally founded United States institutions (representative democracy, capitalism, Protestant faith) and guided America for its first three hundred years. Extreme multiculturalists take this a step further and assign mostly negative connotations to the "Eurocentric" American civilization, blaming our country for most of the world's evils (racism, sexism, heterosexism, imperialism, and destruction of the environment). These extremists aggressively attack traditional American culture (and the white heterosexual males that represent it) as the source of all oppression, abuse, and hegemony. The Marxist philosophy that underlies this is clear—dividing the world into "oppressed" and "oppressors," "exploited" and "exploiting," "abused" and "abusing." The Establishment—white, male, heterosexual—is presented as having all the power and the "people of color," women, homosexuals as power victims. The object, then, is to take power, wealth, prestige, honor, and dignity from this Establishment and transfer it to the poor, nonwhite, nonmale, nonstraight, etc. The mainstream media and much of American higher education advance this multicultural worldview, as James Davison Hunt's classic book *Culture Wars* shows.

Jefferson would disagree. He liked Western civilization. He thought that Greek, Roman, Judeo-Christian, Western European culture was the source of most of what was best in America (notions of individual rights, the innate worth and dignity of humanity, limited government, moral values, a benevolent God, respect of property, technological progress, etc.), which some other civilizations (Muslim, Asian, African) lacked. It's not that we shouldn't study those other civilizations (Jefferson himself did extensive studies of Native American languages and cultures), it's just that T. J. thought Western civilization was superior in some ways.

The main difference for him was the emphasis on the *individual* in the Western heritage. The whole idea of defining people by their culture, race, class, religion, was oppressive to him. He once said that if he could only go to heaven in a group, he would rather not go. Humans are distinct individuals, created by God with unique personalities, gifts, talents, and abilities. To identify them wholly with their race, gender, class, religion, or sexual orientation is demeaning and insulting. And in its own way, racist. Jefferson looked at people as individuals, not categories. And in the Western heritage that he preferred (in the philosophies of Aristotle, St. Augustine, the Bible, John Locke, and Francis Bacon), this individual importance was emphasized (over the more "group"-oriented Eastern cultures). And the United States of America was the one nation on earth that strove to realize that ideal. When a person from any other country in the world came to America, he or she became an "American." If someone outside Japan became a citizen of Japan, he or she did not become Japanese; if you got British citizenship, you would not be considered British; if you moved to Nigeria, you would never be considered Nigerian. Only in America (or, for Jews of all nations, Israel) do you truly adopt the nationality of the country when you gain citizenship there.

Thus, Jefferson would find multicultural attempts to separate Americans into distinctive groups pathetic: it denies each person's individuality, and it denies America's real melting-pot nature. He would find ridiculous the "politically correct" agenda in American universities to have separate women's studies, gay and lesbian studies, Afro-American studies programs; the *Ms.* magazine rule that articles on lesbians can only be written by lesbians; the uproar by witches that the Massachusetts committee planning the three-hundred-year commemoration of the Salem witch trials didn't have a certified witch on it.

Jefferson ridiculed this multicultural "groupism" that puts individuals in categories and then idolizes their cultural past when he denounced the "Wabash Prophet," a Native American cult leader who encouraged American Indians to return to their supposed ancient traditions and separate themselves from all other United States cultures. In a letter to John Adams, he wrote:

> The Wabash Prophet is more rogue than fool, if to be a rogue is not the greatest of all follies. He arose to notice . . . [and] his declared object was the reformation of his red brethren, and their return to their pristine manner of living. He pretended to be in constant communication with the Great Spirit; that he was instructed by Him to make known to the Indians that they were created by Him distinct from the whites, of different natures, for different purposes, and placed under different circumstances . . . that they must return from all the ways of the whites to the habits and opinions of their forefathers; they must not eat the flesh of hogs, of bullocks, of sheep, etc. . . . they must not make bread of wheat . . . they must not wear linen nor woolen, but dress like their fathers in the skins and furs of animals; they must not drink ardent spirits . . .

Sounds just like the exclusivist multiculturalists seeking to separate ethnic groups from American culture based in individual interests, achievements, and contributions.

Jefferson would think the real victims in multicultural education the ones who buy into it, destroying both their individuality and the true melting-pot blending of real American culture. An Asian-American, Frank Wu, wrote of the negative effects of even-positive "group stereotypes" in the *Chronicle of Higher Education*. He cites the *Doonesbury* cartoon where an Asian father is asked the reason for his daughter's academic success; he replies, "Asian virtues of family values and hard work"; the other father retorts, "But doesn't that give her an unfair advantage?" Wu advises, as Jefferson would, "a balance between keeping some differences and overcoming others if we are to achieve a society that is tolerant of difference and fair to us all." This is why the world is beating a path to America's door. The "best and brightest" in India, Africa, Asia, the Middle East, the Philippines, all over the world, want to move to the United States. Why? Because here they believe they will not be Asians, Africans, etc., but Americans. And they will be, unless the multiculturalists completely control education. They will be Americans. And older Americans cannot deny that to them. Just because my family came to New England in the 1640s doesn't mean the Sheldons are "more American" than an Asian or Middle Easterner gaining citizenship in the 1990s. And that reflects Jefferson's hope for America. He encouraged Italian, French, and Irish immigration to the United States.

American public education is frequently attacked for not realizing the goals set out for it by Jefferson. The most basic purpose of Jeffersonian public education was to give elemental skills of reading, writing, and arithmetic to all the American people, making them capable of becoming active, intelligent citizens. On this fundamental level American public schools have seemed to fail. Scholastic Aptitude Test scores among all American students fell 73 points from 1960 to 1993. This while spending on primary and secondary education rose 200 percent. But there seems to be no correlation between spending on education and student success: the top-ranked state in SAT scores (Iowa) is twenty-seventh in expenditures per pupil, while the top state in spending (New Jersey) is thirty-ninth in SAT scores. Much of the failure of American schools may not be due to the schools themselves, but to a general social decline (worsening economic conditions, loss of family stability, rise in crime, etc.). As one writer on education put it: "The American culture increasingly promotes instant gratification over hard work, discipline and deferred benefit."

As mentioned earlier, a 1940 survey of teachers on the top ten problems in the schools included talking out of turn, chewing gum, making noise, running in the halls, cutting in line, and littering. A similar survey in 1990 listed drug abuse, alcohol abuse, pregnancy, suicide, rape, robbery, and assault. Clearly, standards of social conduct have changed. Albert Shanker, president of the American Federation of Teachers, once remarked that "ninety-five percent of the kids who go to college in the United States would not be admitted to college anywhere else in the world." Again, this may not be the fault of the many dedicated teachers, but the general social decline in America. Author James A. Michener writes, "Today, there are drugs and gangs and unprecedented violence. There is the incessant influence of TV, heightening peer pressure to regard fashion and style, for example, as the highest values to which a young person can aspire . . . the eight or ten hours a week my generation spent reading books are superseded by the 30 hours modern kids spend at the television set. The difference produces a radically different set of values." Look at MTV.

Still, some recent reforms in public education, many with distinctly Jeffersonian characteristics, have been successful in reversing the decline in American schooling. In Milwaukee, elementary schools' reading performance was increased, illiteracy dropping from 55 percent in 1979 to 30 percent in 1985 and math illiteracy dropping from 42 percent to 18 percent. Several other regions in

America have developed innovative teaching programs that Jefferson would approve. The HOTS (Higher-Order Thinking Skills) program employs computers for problem solving, student dramatization to improve verbal skills, Socratic questioning, and metacognitive learning to replace remedial-reading labs in grades four to six. A "Reading Recovery" program uses individual tutors to foster first-grade students' reading skills. Vanderbilt's "Anchored Instruction" improves problem-solving skills of low achievers. A Yale University plan uses social and psychological services and encourages parental involvement and active learning; it has shown success in Connecticut and Maryland schools.

All of these innovations Jefferson would applaud, as he would recent reforms in public education giving authority back to the local area and school (decentralization), and public involvement through businesses, churches, and universities. Both basic and advanced cognitive skills Jefferson saw as essential to an intelligent, active democratic citizenry; and those skills, for him, are best exercised locally.

So Jefferson would see hope for American public education, proving the reforming, democratic spirit is not completely lost.

Jefferson's ideal for public education in America was to provide a classical education for every child regardless of wealth or background. His plan for public education in Virginia stated as its goal to "provide an education adapted to the years, to the capacity, and to the condition of everyone" by developing the "worth and genius" of each child, regardless of wealth, birth, or "other accidental condition." The idea was to have society at large pay for the education of every child—as much as the intelligence of each would advance them—all the way through university. The Virginia public education system that Jefferson designed shows this concern for a classical foundation serving progressive ends.

Into the eighteenth-century Virginia society that restricted education to the upper classes (through private tutors), Jefferson devised a system of education, publicly funded and administered, appropriate to a republican citizenry. All people were to receive the rudiments of education, "to illuminate, as far as practicable, the minds of the people at large," with skills necessary for the common transactions of life and the duties and rights of citizens. This included reading, writing, arithmetic, history (ancient and modern), and morals. This would be at public expense, and every American citizen would attend for three years. The next level of public schools for Jefferson would be the county grammar schools, where Latin, Greek, English, geography and higher mathematics would be taught. Every year, rigorous "impartial examinations" would be given each child finishing the Elementary School to determine which, among the "best and most promising genius and disposition" (but too poor to afford it), would go on to these public grammar schools at public expense. Then, out of this county grammar school class, the best student would be selected annually to continue for four more years of "high school." From among the graduates of this elite group, the brightest 50 percent would go on to the public university, where "all the useful sciences" (physics, philosophy, ethics, economics) would be taught them for three years. The overall purpose of this state education system, for Jefferson, was "to provide an education adapted to the years, to the capacity, and to the condition of everyone and directed to their freedom and happiness," by nurturing the "worth and genius" in people, "regardless of wealth, birth or other accidental condition." It was, for Jefferson, essential for the system to be publicly funded, so that "those talents which nature has sown as liberally among the poor as the rich, but which perish without use if not sought for and cultivated" would be developed amongst all Americans. On such a classical, public education system, managed by the states, Jefferson believed the future political and economic order of America would be based.

As he wrote of Montesquieu: "He considers political virtue . . . the energetic principle of a democratic republic . . . and shows that every government should provide that its energetic principle should be the object of the education of its youth." This educational system would do that by (1) teaching every citizen the basics of knowledge, equipping them to intelligently order their own lives and participate in self-government by electing the most talented and virtuous as political leaders and representatives, and (2) providing advanced learning to the most talented and gifted (the "natural aristocracy") who should serve as leaders in politics, business, law, and other disciplines. He wished to see an educational system in America securing the happiness of all classes of society:

> It is generally true that people are happiest whose laws are best . . . in proportion as those who form and administer them are wise and honest . . . it becomes expedient for promoting the public happiness that those persons, whom nature hath endowed with genius and virtue, should be rendered by liberal education worthy to receive and able to guard the sacred deposit of the rights and liberties of their fellow citizens . . .

Without such a public school system, Jefferson feared the leadership of society would be taken over by the "weak or wicked"—the false aristocracy of wealth and family connections. University training was to cap this system, and his design for the University of Virginia reveals this.

Again, the classics formed the foundation of the curriculum. He divided it into these areas: ancient languages (Hebrew, Latin, and Greek), mathematics, physics, natural philosophy, natural history, medicine, law and ideology, and government. He sought for faculty from the finest European universities: a classicist from Oxford, a mathematician from Cambridge, an anatomist from Edinburgh, and a modern languages scholar from the Continent. But the most significant import was the free spirit of inquiry at the University of Virginia. There was to be no "politically correct" speech code restricting ideas or discourse. "This institution," he wrote, "will be based on the illimitable freedom of the human mind. For here we are not afraid to follow truth wherever it may lead, nor to tolerate any error so long as reason is left free to combat it." That standard of academic freedom and inquiry is literally carved in stone at the University of Virginia in Charlottesville. And this would benefit the whole country as the most gifted doctors, teachers, lawyers, scientists, ministers, writers, and businesspeople would be discovered by the educational system and given the training they need. This would enhance both individual and social "freedom and happiness." On such democratic education, he wrote, "the principal foundations of future order will be laid."

It is in the interest of everyone that the brightest, most hard-working students be recognized, encouraged, and trained. "The object is to bring into action that mass of talents which lies buried in poverty . . . and thus give activity to a mass of mind." Without good education the nation will be robbed of this talent, and the costs of "ignorance and vice" will be much higher (in crime and dissipation) than the taxes charged to provide high-quality education. It will also prevent political tyranny, for Jefferson, as he wrote: "The most effectual means of preventing the perversion of power into tyranny are to illuminate . . . the minds of the people."

Everything from crime to teen suicide and political extremists like the Modern Militia might be ascribed by Jefferson to ignorance and the frustrations born of ignorance.

Jefferson would prefer that this education of Americans—both of classical knowledge and occupational skills—be public, that is, financed by taxes and controlled democratically. But, if those noble ends are thwarted in the public schools (by political movements: "multiculturalism," "politically correct" speech, "gay" studies, Clinton's national curriculum, etc.), Jefferson would support private schools like those he himself attended that *did* serve the interests of traditional education, occupational preparation, and quality public service.

Nine

HEALTH CARE

"Nature and kind nursing save a much greater propor-
tion . . . at a smaller expense, and with less abuse."

—THOMAS JEFFERSON

Thomas Jefferson had little personal illness. He was blessed with remarkably good health all his life, right up to a few weeks before his death at age eighty-three. "I have been more fortunate . . . in the article of health," he wrote. "My hearing is distinct [I have been] . . . so free from catarrhs [colds] that I have not had one (in the breast, I mean) on an average of eight or ten years through life . . . A fever of more than twenty-four hours I have not had above two or three times in my life." At age seventy-six, Jefferson proclaimed, "I enjoy good health."

Jefferson shared the common eighteenth-century suspicion of physicians, joking that if a doctor was visiting the neighborhood, buzzards would immediately begin circling above it. He claimed "the sun" was his great physician—being outdoors in the fresh, warm air. He believed in what today we would call holistic medicine—integrating physical with emotional and spiritual. Like the Native Americans he admired in so many ways, he emphasized the healing power of nature, the *vis medicatrix naturae,* or our body's natural defense and recuperative abilities. As he wrote to Dr. Caspar Wistas in 1807, "the humane physician" should keep his remedies to a minimum, relying most on the patient's natural recovery powers and following the first principle of the Hippocratic oath: "Do no harm." Jefferson advised the young doctor:

> Having been so often a witness to the salutary efforts which nature makes to re-establish the disordered functions, he should rather trust to their action, than hazard the interruption of that, and a greater derangement of the system, by conjectural experiments on a machine so complicated and so unknown as the human body, and a subject so sacred as human life . . . I would wish the young practitioner [be a] quiet spectator of the operations of nature, giving them fair play by a well-regulated regimen, and by all the aid they can derive from the excitement of good spirits and hope in the patient.

Although Jefferson himself was free of illness, it was all around him all his life. Sickness and death were constant companions in early Virginia, taking his young father when Thomas was just fourteen, removing several of his brothers and sisters, snatching away his wife and domestic happiness when he was in his thirties, killing four of his six children in infancy, and frequently laying low his large family and body of slaves at Monticello. His favorite slave, Jupiter, was killed by the medicine administered by a black witch doctor.

Jefferson attributed his health to healthy habits: a diet consisting of little meat or fat, abstinence from tobacco and alcohol (taking only occasional light wine, after St. Paul's advice to Timothy), lots of vegetables, and the regular exercise of walking and horseback riding. Walking, for Jefferson, was the best of exercise, and best done for two hours a day, in all weather, at a regular time, and without a book or other distractions (except, perhaps, in the country, a gun), as it relaxes the mind. A diet like that of the Indians, of mostly grains and fruits and vegetables, was the healthiest, for Jefferson. He wrote:

> I have lived temperately, eating little animal food, and that not as an aliment, so much as a condiment for the vegetables, which constitute my principal diet. I double, however, the Doctor's glass and a half of wine, and even triple it with a friend; but halve its effects by drinking the weak wines only. The ardent wines I cannot drink, nor do I use ardent spirits in any form . . . and my breakfast is of tea and coffee.

Jefferson complained of the "loathsome and fatal effect" of hard liquor and of the "wretchedness" of tobacco. Avoidance of harmful substances combined with "active exercise" would lead to a healthy mind and body, for Jefferson. This surprisingly contemporary advice for healthy living reveals Jefferson's characteristic wisdom. Like current physicians' emphasis on prevention of disease (not just treatment), Jefferson would see much of Americans' ailments due to unhealthy lifestyles: fat- and salt-filled food (especially "fast food"), excessive alcohol, lack of exercise in an increasingly sedentary society, and ever-mounting stress. On the matter of stress, Jefferson firmly believed in vacations—long ones. He insisted, as president, on taking a two-month summer vacation in the mountains of Virginia, to escape the stresses of executive work and the unhealthful heat and humidity of Washington, D.C. Business concerns, he wrote, "induce us to prepare leaving this place during the two sickly months, as well as for the purposes of health . . ."

Stress was the cause of Jefferson's only lifelong ailments: migraine headaches and persistent diarrhea. He also became depressed and reclusive during periods of intense public criticism. The headaches, which he said caused him "the most excruciating pain," struck him most often when he faced a personal or political crisis. The diarrhea also erupted during times of great stress. His doctor, Benjamin Rush, advised Jefferson to discontinue his lifelong regimen of bathing his feet in ice water every morning (which T. J. claimed kept him from getting colds). Dr. Rush wrote him, "The bowels sympathize with the feet above any other external part of the body, and suffer in a peculiar manner from the effects of cold water on them." Dr. William Eustic of Boston also encouraged regular exercise on horseback. With this therapy, Jefferson was cured of this "visceral complaint" for many years.

The only other physical problems Mr. Jefferson suffered from were a broken right wrist (which he injured jumping over a fence in France while pursuing Maria Cosway), which never healed properly and tormented him the rest of his life, making writing painful and difficult; and, in old age, rheumatism and urinary tract infections.

But Jefferson remained active and healthy up to the last few weeks of his life. Just before July 4, 1826, the old ailments of diarrhea and urinary infection combined to lay him low in his bed. His mind remained clear until the last day or so, as he conversed with family members. His grandson listened to Jefferson's recollections of Revolutionary times, which he described "in his usual cheerful manner, insensibly diverting my mind from his dying condition." Dr. Dunglison, university professor of medicine, attended him. Near the end he suddenly awoke and asked if Mr. Hatch, the minister of the church he attended, was there, as Jefferson wished to see him. Slipping into delirium, Jefferson sat up in his sleep and went through the motion of writing something. On July 3, he briefly awoke and asked, "Is it the Fourth?"—his last words. The next day—the fiftieth anniversary of the Declaration of Independence—Jefferson died at one o'clock in the afternoon. John Adams, the Revolutionary comrade and friend of old age, but political nemesis, died a few hours later. Adams's dying words, "Jefferson survives," were to become prophetic. Adams was always a little off on the facts, but profound on the *Geist*.

Two days before his death, Jefferson told his daughter Patsy to look in a desk drawer for a note for her. Patsy was his oldest daughter, his companion throughout his adult life, and his most beloved relative after his wife. He left her this poem:

A Death-bed Adieu from Th.J. to M.R.

Life's visions are vanished, its dreams are no more;
Dear friends of my bosom, why bathed in tears?
I go to my fathers, I welcome the shore
Which crowns all my hopes or which buries my cares.
Then farewell, my dear, my lov'd daughter, adieu!
The last pang of life is in parting from you!
Two seraphs await me long shrouded in death;
I will bear them your love on my last parting breath.

Like so many of Jefferson's remedies for social ills, his ideas on care for the sick mix publicly funded with privately administered programs. Jefferson would oppose both a highly centralized, national health care plan and extensive reliance on large hospitals. The American system of smaller regional hospitals treating common problems, with larger, specialized university hospitals taking the most serious cases, would make sense to Jefferson. The problem with liberal health care reforms, like Clinton's, is their over-centralization of care and attendant regulation and expense. Liberal plans promise secure health care for all Americans, but the *New York Times* reported that even the guarantees of Medicaid left 2 million Americans untreated in 1992 because Medicaid reimbursements were too low. The nationalized medical system of Canada has led to rationing, waiting lists, and shortages. Canadian heart surgeons estimate that the statistical risk of dying on the waiting list now exceeds the risk of dying on the operating table.

The purported simplicity of a Clinton-like plan would actually complicate America's already complex system of doctors, insurers, and government regulations. Even Democrats acknowledged that the cost-saving projections of Clinton's health plan were pure fantasy and that, in fact, the policy's costs would skyrocket like other federal entitlements.

But the real fear of a major readjustment of the medical delivery system in America was the reduction of quality of care. Medical services in the United States are the best in the world. By "throwing out the baby with the bathwater," the Clinton plan threatened to "kill the goose that laid the golden egg." Overregulation and price controls discourage the best students from going into the medical profession and ultimately harm everyone's health care. Punitive measures against pharmaceutical companies discourage investment in new technology and drugs. Most Americans should have private physicians and private insurance. But the dictatorial control that insurance companies have over benefits and beneficiaries (including now using genetic research to weed out probable "bad risks") would disturb Jefferson. This is one instance where state regulation (over a national industry) is ineffective. The poor should receive publicly subsidized health care. Jefferson believed that most care of the sick could be undertaken by the family and recommended that those without families should be placed in the home of "a good farmer," who would be paid by the state to care for the patient.

Now, when many American families have no one staying at home (i.e., they're all working), this may be difficult to replicate. But the principle of publicly subsidized, privately administered health care in the home favors the growing "home health care" industry, as the most Jeffersonian solution.

In an article entitled "Many Things Old Are New Again," *USA Today* reported that Jeffersonian-style simplicity is on the rise in America. The aging baby boom generation will prompt greater and cheaper home health care, including doctors making house calls. As the elderly find it harder to travel to the physician's office (and wait interminably in the waiting room, where one could easily die of boredom), the nurse or doctor making personal calls on the sick makes sense. Seeing the patient's living environment can also help the health care professional diagnose illnesses from poor diet or allergy problems. Taking the person's pulse is still a major method of determining basic health, especially of the heart, and employs "high touch" personal contact over "high tech" impersonal treatment. In St. Paul, Minnesota, a Neighborhood Nurse program provides regular at-home checking on, and care for, elderly residents. A neighborhood association organizes visitations of younger people to elderly neighbors. For example, Jo Ann Mason visits eighty-year-old Mary Knight, helping with light housework, bathing, and errands. The widow remarked, "Hopefully I can avoid a nursing home for the rest of my life."

Staying at home keeps up the spirits and sense of independence and familiarity—just Jefferson's prescription. Recently the Robert Wood Johnson Foundation gave $25,000 to various churches, synagogues, and social service agencies to support volunteer services to the American elderly. In rural Arizona Faith in Action volunteers deliver medicine and groceries to older people who live in remote regions. In Decatur, Alabama, a Jeffersonian plan funded by the federal Corporation for National Service, involves paying stipends to the poor ($3,800) to help homebound senior citizens with housekeeping and errands. It is estimated that helping sixty elderly people stay out of nursing homes saves taxpayers $2 million annually.

In the future, American medical care will become even more Jeffersonian, scholars predict. At-home computers will provide diagnostic services for local hospitals; visiting, independent nurses will treat most Americans in the comfort of their residences; pharmacists will gain more authority to advise and prescribe medicines. Even though surgery pays the highest doctor's salaries, nonintrusive medical "scans" will increase in the future (a *Newsweek* article said, "Anytime a doctor sticks something into someone, he receives a bonus"). More personal, patient-attentive care will expand, partly due to more female doctors entering the profession (female patients say, "Quality is a doctor who talks to me before he tells me to take my clothes off").

Ten

CRIME

> *"It frequently happens that wicked and dissolute men,
> resigning themselves to the dominion of inordinate
> passions, commit violations on the lives, liberties and
> property of others . . . government would be defective
> in its principal purpose, were it not to restrain such
> criminal acts, by inflicting punishment on those who
> perpetrate them."*
>
> —THOMAS JEFFERSON, 1779

Jefferson would express both the liberal concern with humane
treatment of criminals and the conservative concern with protection of the victims of crime by swift and sure punishment.

Thomas Jefferson did not personally experience crime, or the
fear of crime that haunts contemporary America. The few incidents
of crime that he experienced tended to be associated with slaves.
Like most white plantation owners in the South, Jefferson complained that black slaves had a propensity to steal (household objects, food, small tools); but Jefferson excused such petty larceny
on the poor and oppressed conditions of slavery. In his *Notes on
the State of Virginia* he wrote:

> That disposition to theft with which they have been branded,
> must be ascribed to their situation and not to any depravity of

the moral sense. The man in whose favor no laws of property exist, probably feels himself less bound to respect those made in favor of others . . . And whether the slave may not as justifiably take a little from one who has taken all from him . . . ? That a change in the relations in which a man is placed should change his ideas of moral right or wrong, is neither new, nor peculiar to the color of the blacks. Homer tells us it was so two thousand six hundred years ago.

Jefferson cannot be accused of "blaming the victim," just as today many liberals explain the disproportionate rate of black crime on those citizens' disadvantaged social and economic conditions. About a third of all black children are born to unmarried women; one in four black men is in prison, paroled, or on probation; black Americans are six times more likely to be murdered than white Americans. Without the murder rate of blacks (mostly by other blacks), the U.S. homicide rate would be that of Luxembourg (one of the lowest in the world).

Jefferson did experience the incidence of black violence against other blacks: one of the few reasons for his ever selling a slave was for black males who habitually assaulted other slaves. And he was acquainted with the connection between drugs (in his time, mostly alcohol) and crime, violence, and dissipation. Such drug-induced violence had, he wrote, created "terrible havoc" among the Indians of Virginia, had been a "fatal infatuation" under which anyone could destroy "his usefulness to society," and led to "ruinous self-indulgence." In contemporary America an estimated 70 percent of prison inmates went into crime to get money for drugs. In a small town in rural Virginia the house burglary rate suddenly jumped from an average of two a year to ten a month. Police discovered a cocaine ring recently established in the little town; when it was busted up, the burglaries stopped. To such criminals who get hooked on drugs and then steal to support their habit, the penalties for crime make little difference. As a drug dealer in Trenton, New Jersey, said, "I was too busy being high to worry."

Jefferson's own family experienced the very connection between crime and drugs, especially the contemporary problem of the link between alcohol addiction and abuse, drunkenness and domestic violence, especially against women. Jefferson's own favorite daughter, Martha, was the victim of an alcohol-enraged violent husband, as was his granddaughter Anne. The latter's early death in 1826 was believed attributable to her husband, a handsome, distinguished man whose drunken rages caused a relative to describe him as "a worthless . . . malignant drunkard." An overseer at Monticello witnessed him beat his wife, once in front of her own mother. Anne would often run away from his violent attacks and take refuge in a hole used for storing potatoes outside. When Anne's brother Thomas Jefferson Randolph confronted husband Bankhead in front of the courthouse in Charlottesville about this abuse of his sister, Bankhead pulled out a long knife and stabbed him several times. Only the interference of Randolph's companion prevented his being murdered. Hearing the news of the stabbing, Jefferson quickly rode his horse down to the town and found the wounded grandson. Jefferson's namesake wrote, "I had been laid on a bale of blankets in the crating room of a store, and had borne myself with proper fortitude; but when he [Jefferson] entered and knelt at my head and wept aloud I was unnerved."

On another occasion, this violent grandson-in-law, Bankhead, was staying up late at Monticello demanding more and more brandy. Finally, Burwell, the most trusted household slave, locked the liquor cabinet and refused to serve Bankhead any more drinks. Flying into a rage, he attacked the recalcitrant servant, but in a darkened room mistook another family member, Thomas Mann Randolph, for Burwell. Randolph seized a fireplace poker and struck Bankhead in the skull, knocking him down and almost killing him. A relative described Anne Bankhead's early death as "happily for herself."

Jefferson's eldest daughter's husband not only beat Martha, causing her to leave him and return to Monticello with her ten children, but his drunken binges caused him to quarrel and fight with many other people in public. He finally went completely mad, and Jefferson cut him entirely out of his will, leaving his daughter in charge of all the property she inherited.

The most notorious criminal elements in Jefferson's clan were two nephews, Lilburn and Isham Lewis, who, living in Kentucky, reportedly killed a black slave, "literally chopped [him] to pieces," it was said. This scandalous murder became legendary to antislavery northern abolitionists and contributed to the passions that led to the Civil War and Emancipation Proclamation. Jefferson's response to this hideous crime is unrecorded.

The drunkenness and violence that existed in Jefferson's extended family were not uncommon in Virginia in the 1700s. In the Puritan-influenced Low Church Anglican commonwealth, laws existed against Sabbath breaking (not attending church at least once a month), public drunkenness, and profanity (swearing in public). In a survey of eighteenth-century Virginia criminal records, most county governments show these to be the three most common violations, and probably by the same offenders! The kindly town drunk, Otis Campbell, in the television series *The Andy Griffith Show* is actually a southern type, although the real McCoy is much meaner and more foulmouthed than "good ol' Otis." The proclivity to shouted profanity and violent outbursts among the culture of poor southern men may explain some of President Clinton's behavior with his wife and associates, where Bill's angry rages gained him the nickname "the Monster." Heavy drinking, quick tempers, lack of self-control, and domestic violence constituted the leading causes of crime in Jefferson's society.

The criminal justice system in his time was equally brutal—inflicting physical mutilation and degrading conditions on prison inmates. Chain gangs, recently revived in some southern penal systems, were ridiculed by Jefferson in his autobiography: "Exhibited as a public spectacle, with shaved heads and mean clothing, work-ing on the high roads, produced in the criminals such a prostration of character, such an abandonment of self-respect, as, instead of reforming, plunged them into the most desperate and hardened depravity of morals and character."

Jefferson would be disappointed and sobered to see that more humane prison conditions in contemporary America have not seemed to soften the character of the incarcerated or made them more amenable to reform. But at least he would not be surprised that many modern crimes are still traceable to alcohol and drug use, domestic violence, and the breakdown of the family structure.

The breakdown in the family and traditional moral values con-tributes to the frustration, hopelessness, and evil that lead to drug use and then crime and violence. Harvard Professor Richard Free-man has found that inner-city youth with a strong religious orien-tation are 54 percent less likely to use drugs and 50 percent less likely to commit crimes.

Jefferson also recognized the economic dimension of crime—the temptation to crime among the desperately poor (see chapter 7, "The Economy and Welfare"). In one sense "crime pays" in America. The chance of being caught and punished is slim: a crim-inal committing a felony has a 1 in 100 chance of serving time in prison (much better odds than the state lottery!). Even if sentenced to prison, the average time served is declining: for robbery, from fifty-seven months in 1986 to thirty-eight months in 1988. Crime pays, but not that well. Harvard Kennedy School Professor Mark Kleiman calculates the average burglar makes fifty dollars an hour; but adding "work time" lost in jail, that goes down to thirty-three cents an hour—"McDonald's pays much better," he says. But many criminal types have trouble finding a job anywhere—even at McDonald's. This explains why drug crime is so common: it is lucrative. Even a small-time street dealer in Washington, D.C., grosses about $50,000 a year.

America has embarked on the largest prison-building campaign in our history. Over the past decade we have doubled our prison population; that is more convicts per capita than any other country on earth. So much for "the land of the free"! Money for prison construction rose four times faster in the last decade than spending on education. Criminal justice majors mushroom in American universities, replacing growth in business majors. But does an increase in prisons work? Higher incarceration rates have slowed the rise of violent crime rates. But a University of Chicago Law School professor said, "Using more prisons to fight crime is like using a mosquito to attack an elephant." More prisons and longer prison sentences seem to satisfy Americans' thirst for vengeance, but they are enormously expensive and not very effective in reducing the crime rate.

In 1776 Jefferson began revision of the laws of Virginia. A large portion of that revised code came under the title "Criminal Law," which gives us a good idea of his ideas on crime and punishment.

The first thing that strikes us about Jefferson's view of crime and punishment is his humane attitude. He wants the punishment to "fit the crime." He realizes that vengeance is a temptation in periods of high crime. But Jefferson rejects the harsh punishments of minor crimes found in England. "In England . . . to steal a hare, is death the first offense." Jefferson is proud that in America stealing a rabbit does not lead to execution. But he is not opposed to the death penalty for serious crimes.

He is not "soft on crime." Just sensible. For treason and murder the penalty should be death and forfeiture of property. Manslaughter should be punished by forfeiture of property (fine) and labor (while in prison). Other crimes (burglary, theft, assault) should be punished by forfeiture, fines, prison, labor in public works (such as mines, dockyards, factories, and roads).

Jefferson advocated another provision of criminal law that is being revived in America today: restitution. This requires criminals to restore the money or property they've stolen or damaged, or "make up" the injury they've inflicted. Several states are taking the property of criminals and giving it to their victims, or making criminals work for the people they've harmed. Jefferson would approve of this as both a way to teach the criminal the cost of his crime and a means of compensating the victim.

Just building more and more prisons or giving out longer and longer sentences would not necessarily punish or reform criminals or recompense victims, and it will lay a heavy financial burden on the public.

Several innovative criminal justice alternatives would appeal to Jefferson as less wasteful of public revenues and more effective in rehabilitating criminals. One program used successfully in Madison, Wisconsin, Newport News, Virginia, and other cities is "community policing." Putting cops back on the street; getting them acquainted with neighborhoods; identifying problems (youth problems, drug rings, gangs, etc.) while they're getting started up rather than after they become full blown; working with law-abiding citizens in a personal way to stop crime rather than answering endless 911 emergency calls after the crime has been committed, all seem to be working to slow crime, even in New York City, which is not even in the top fifty cities anymore with regard to violent crime. Such direct, personal police work resembles the county sheriffs of Jefferson's Virginia (or Mayberry, North Carolina).

Alternatives to prison for nonviolent offenders have been shown to save money and help criminals (especially drug addicts) to be rehabilitated. In many programs a parole officer visits the convict under "house arrest" on a weekly basis to test him for drugs, encourage his progress, and monitor his compliance. Surveillance can be done electronically. Such programs are shown to be more effective in reducing repeat crimes and can reduce the annual cost to taxpayers of keeping a prisoner from $25,000 to $6,000. Jefferson would approve.

Jefferson would not be soft on crime; he would be sensible and just.

STATES' RIGHTS

*"I believe the States can best govern our home con-
cerns."*

—THOMAS JEFFERSON, 1823

Jefferson would have applauded the Gingrich-led Republican
Congress and its returning many public programs to the states. For
him, most of our "home concerns"—domestic policy—from welfare
to health care, from police to art to school lunches, are best governed at the state and local levels. Jefferson wrote: "the States
should preserve their sovereignty in whatever concerns themselves . . ."

Thomas Jefferson loved his state of Virginia. He called it his
"country." The rolling green hills of the Piedmont, the sandy shores
of the Tidewater, the rugged mountain cliffs of the Blue Ridge and
Appalachians, the graceful wide rivers snaking through grassy val-
leys, the glorious expanse of the Shenandoah, all fed Jefferson's
affection for his native land.

"My native state is endeared to me by every tie which can attach
the human heart," he wrote in 1809. Family ties rooted him to
Virginia's origins: his mother came from the noble Randolph clan
of aristocrats; his father, Peter, making the first map of the commonwealth, symbolically created its boundaries.

Even when away from his beloved Virginia for long periods of public service, in Philadelphia, Paris, and Washington, D.C., Jefferson longed for his mountaintop home, Monticello.

> Dear Monticello . . . where has nature spread so rich a mantle . . . ? Mountains, forests, rocks, rivers! With what majesty do we there ride above the storms! How sublime to look down into the workhouse of nature, to see her clouds, hail, snow, rain, thunder, all fabricated at our feet! And the glorious sun when rising, as if out of a distant water, just gilding the tops of the mountains, and giving life to all nature!

When contemplating retirement, he confessed, "All my wishes end, where I hope my days will end, at Monticello. Too many scenes of happiness mingle themselves with all the recollections of my native woods and fields . . ." Jefferson's love of nature in Virginia made him America's first environmentalist.

The affection and regard Jefferson held for Virginia was shared by other citizens of eighteenth-century America: in Connecticut, Massachusetts, New York, Delaware, Pennsylvania, and other states, where, without the geographic mobility of our time, men and women identified with their state rather than with the nation. This explains why Jefferson, as many others, believed in states' rights—the retention of political control at the state and local level. The independent states, he wrote, "like the planets revolving around their common sun [the federal government], acting and acted upon according to their respective weights and distances, will produce that beautiful equilibrium on which our Constitution is founded . . ." The Tenth Amendment to the Constitution, for Thomas Jefferson, guaranteed states' rights. This leaves the federal government to take care of international affairs, foreign relations, and the concerns between states. A president should primarily know how to wisely conduct foreign relations. (A joke about presidential candidate Michael Dukakis was that his idea of foreign relations was New Hampshire.)

Jefferson, like contemporary conservatives, thought that states have different needs—and those living in the states know them best. An intrusive federal presence in domestic legislation too easily becomes wasteful, despotic, and annoying. Washington, D.C., is too easily taken over by special interests who manipulate the state and local programs to serve their benefit. Jefferson believed it would be harder to deceive the state governments to do stupid things than it would a remote, corrupt national government. The fact that most states have constitutional provisions forbidding deficit spending (requiring a balanced budget) would prove this point, for Jefferson.

Jefferson's theory of federalism involved several tiers or levels of government, each performing the functions it did best:

> The way to have good and safe government, is not to trust it all to one, but to divide it among the many, distributing to every one exactly the functions he is competent to. Let the national government be entrusted with the defense of the nation, and its foreign and federal relations; the State governments with the civil rights, laws, police, and administration of what concerns the states generally; the counties with the local concerns of the counties . . . It is by dividing and subdividing these republics from the great national one down through all its subordinations, until it ends in the administration of every man's farm by himself; by placing under everyone what his own eye may superintend, that all will be done for the best.

This sounds so contemporary! As America shifts power and control from the central federal government in Washington back to the states in matters of welfare, education, police and prisons, health care, civil rights (affirmative action), and regulation of utilities, this

Jeffersonian formula seems to make wonderful sense. And the "cement" of this whole pyramid of republics in American federalism remained, for Jefferson, the direct participation of each citizen, that at some time in their lives, at some level of government, whether city council, ward superintendent, neighborhood crime watch committee, county supervisor, local school board, state legislator, court jury, congressional representative, district judge, or president, every American would serve. This would produce the dedication to country and intelligence of citizenship that T. J. thought would preserve American democracy.

An apathetic, self-absorbed, consumerist, narrow-minded population for Jefferson would lead to an American fit only for (as he put it) "sinning and suffering." But an active, experienced, intelligent citizenry would logically produce the "wise and frugal government, which shall restrain men from injuring one another, which shall leave them otherwise free to regulate their own pursuits of industry and improvement." Such a proud, capable American would "let the heart be torn out of his body sooner than his power be wrested from him by a Caesar or a Bonaparte." A safe republic. Strong. Solid. Sturdy. But impossible unless the federal government accepted the fact that "the states themselves have principal care of our persons, our property and our reputations." That is, states' rights.

For Jefferson didn't just fear that big government in Washington over all domestic programs would turn the average American into a mindless "automaton" (his word), a timid sheep, but that concentrated political power would turn political leaders into "wolves" (in sheep's clothing) devouring the helpless, common people. Remember the old welfare system? In the name of "compassion" and "helping the poor," trapping millions of Americans in degrading poverty, dependence on the federal government, fearful, timid, confused, locked into generations of misery, leading to crime and drugs and death? And yet, dependent upon the very system that enslaved and oppressed them, desperately voting for the party that put them there, for fear of the alternative (relying on themselves and their fellow citizens)? Jefferson wouldn't have believed it possible, in America.

And when those "wolves" were not self-righteously manipulating the poor and helpless with schemes that enslaved and controlled them, Jefferson saw them manipulating the system for private gain. Profit. Wealth. Using the government to fleece the middle-class taxpaying sheep. Jefferson got a preview of this with Hamilton and his fiscally clever Federalist friends. Corruption. Remember the savings and loan scandal? Jefferson would say they took a page out of Alex Hamilton's Treasury book. Or National Bank book.

Hamilton is the guy who "helped" the states by advocating their turning over all their Revolutionary War debts to the federal government. Sort of like "consolidating your loans." Be careful about people who want to help you with your debts, Jefferson warned.

Jefferson saw the Hamiltonian system of combined business, banking, and central government as reintroducing the corrupt British system we'd just gotten rid of! "All the administrative laws," he wrote, "were shaped on the model of England . . . and to be warped, in practice, into all the principles and pollutions of their favorite English model [e.g., the Bank of England and the East India Company] . . . For Hamilton was not only a monarchist, but for monarchy bottomed in corruption."

For Jefferson, political corruption follows Aristotle's definition of people using the power of the government for private, selfish gain rather than for the common good. Whitewater. Such corruption, for the Greeks, and T. J., flourished in a distant, centralized regime, remote from the common people, filled with clever, sophisticated folks whose "greed and avarice" led them to shamelessly and cynically filch money from the average citizen. Every capital city could become the Court of Versailles, a Vanity Fair of wealth, greed, pomp, and corruption. Hamilton's Federalist Washington, D.C., contained such a "base scramble" for public largesse, a "detestable game" of "greedy creditors and speculators," whose actions, for Jefferson, allowed "immense sums to be filched from the poor and ignorant."

Such an abuse of power may occur in state and local governments, but not as frequently or on the magnitude or scale of a centralized national government. Simply because state governments are geographically nearer to most citizens, the public can scrutinize them better. But in Washington, Jefferson wrote, most leaders had to "occupy themselves and their capital in a species of gambling, destructive of morality, and which has introduced its poison into the government itself." And Jefferson nearly wept when he observed how many in the early American Republic succumbed to Hamilton's tricks and temptations. "And with grief and shame it must be acknowledged that his machine was not without effect; that even in this, the birth of our government, some members were found sordid enough to bend their duty to their interests, and look after personal rather than public good." Are you listening, Bill? Al?

The solution, according to T. J., was to return as many federal programs, policies, and guidelines as possible back to the states. His fear of federal usurpation of power and corruption of politics became so severe that he advocated secession from the Union. The South followed his advice fifty years later. The slavery issue was only a small part of the controversy. In 1816 Jefferson wrote that he saw the alternatives as "1., licentious commerce and gambling speculations for a few, with eternal war for the many; or, 2., restricted commerce, peace, and steady occupations for all." He continued, "If any State in the Union will declare that it prefers separation with the first alternative, to a continuance in union without it, I have no hesitation in saying 'let us separate.' " Here, Jefferson is referring to the threat made repeatedly by *northern* states to secede from the Union, but of course it was the southern states that finally did so. The northern victory in the Civil War forced the southern Confederacy to remain in the United States. In the end, Jefferson would probably have supported the southern Confederacy's secession, but now would agree with the advantages of a continued union (the South having a civilizing effect on the rest of the nation!). Still, he would hope for a return to states' control over most domestic policies (economy, welfare, education, crime).

The real imposition of federal tyranny over the states (and individuals) didn't come until the 1930s with FDR's New Deal. In one liberal Supreme Court ruling (*Wickard v. Filburn,* 1942) the Court decided that a farmer's wheat grown on his own land and consumed by his own family and livestock was part of "interstate commerce" and therefore could be regulated by the federal government under the Constitution's Commerce Clause! Such extreme usurpation of private property rights and federal control over domestic policy would have shocked Jefferson. He might have asked when the day would come when a resident of Virginia might have to ask permission of the federal government before he sneezed, since the germs might blow over into Kentucky, rendering the act liable to congressional control under the Interstate Commerce Clause.

Again, Jefferson's solution to the absurdity, tyranny, corruption, and emasculation of federal power is to return control to the states over domestic policy and to individuals over economic matters. Recent American history has shown several attempts at just this devolution of political power to the decentralized state governments. Professor David Walker at the University of Connecticut examines three such attempts since the 1960s ("New Federalism" I–III) under Presidents Nixon, Reagan, and Clinton. He finds that next to FDR's New Deal in the 1930s, Lyndon Johnson's "aggressive national assertion of policy leadership by both the political and the judicial branches of the Federal government" was the greatest concentration of central power in American history.

Republican presidents thereafter tried to cut back on this growth of federal power by sending authority and money back to the states through general revenue sharing, block grants, and reduction of federal programs. Despite these efforts by Nixon and Reagan, Walker finds "the soaring growth in entitlements, thanks in part to their indexation, combined to produce the earliest example of an ambivalent federalism" where campaigns to reduce the Washington role combined with increased Washington presence.

Ironically, a liberal Democratic president, Bill Clinton, achieved more real decentralization of political power through a combination of his "significant sensitivity to state and local interests" (as a former governor of Arkansas) and the Republican Party's control of Congress under Newt Gingrich. The GOP's Contract with America helped nudge President Clinton to less federal government by passing laws that required cost analysis, risk assessment, and early state-local consultation before new federal regulations could be implemented. The Republicans' pledge to have "smaller government, lower taxes, less power in Washington, and greater emphasis on individual responsibility and personal morality" led to legislation consolidating federal programs, welfare and legal reforms, budget cuts, and return of jurisdiction to states over many domestic policies (welfare, education, family law, and criminal justice). Gingrich and Company didn't succeed in cutting all environmental programs, or abolishing three departments, sixty-nine commissions, thirteen agencies, and 284 programs, but it did effect radical change in federal-state relations. By outlawing unfunded federal mandates to states, "the Republican Revolution" ushered in a clarion call for states' rights.

The dramatic change in the American welfare system in 1996 is a good example. The Republican bill signed by President Clinton ended the sixty-year federal government–controlled and guaranteed welfare system. It ended welfare as a federal entitlement. Cuts in welfare to legal immigrants and food stamp programs will save the federal government $55 billion over the next six years. States are given a lump sum from the federal government to run their own welfare programs. The heads of most families on welfare must find work within two years or lose benefits. If able-bodied welfare recipients cannot find private sector employment in two years, they can be required to do public service work. No one can now receive more than five years of welfare in a lifetime. Unmarried mothers on welfare must identify the fathers of their children or possibly lose 25 percent of their welfare benefits, and unmarried teen mothers may receive welfare only if they remain at home and in school. States are allowed to make these general federal guidelines more or less stringent, but if they don't reduce welfare caseloads by 20 percent by 1997 and 50 percent by 2002, they have their federal block grants reduced. And states must deny welfare to convicted drug users and dealers.

Overall, the 1996 welfare reform represents the greatest return to states' rights and Jeffersonian notions of federalism in recent times. It respects the wisdom, compassion, and jurisdiction of the states. It acknowledges that different states have different needs, resources, and cultures, which cannot be dictated to by a massive central government. It recognizes that involving citizens at the state and local levels in important policy makes them more committed, virtuous "owners" of those policies.

But this doesn't mean Jefferson was a weak, laissez-faire conservative. A William F. Buckley, Jr. Like a liberal, Jefferson endorsed extensive public services—in education, welfare, health care, public improvements, etc. He just thought those extensive public services were best developed and administered at the state and local levels, where people (presumably) know the problems and how best to solve them. Sound simple? It is! Liberals, like the Federalists Jefferson knew, often complicate issues to confuse people.

Still, when the tyranny comes from organizations (monopolies, trusts, international conglomerates) against which states cannot effectively protect individuals or the environment, Jefferson would see a role for the national government serving the public good.

Twelve

FREEDOM OF SPEECH

"Truth is the proper and sufficient antagonist to error, and has nothing to fear from the conflict, unless by human interposition, disarmed of her natural weapons, free argument and debate."

—THOMAS JEFFERSON, 1779

Jefferson was in favor of free speech even when it produced offensive language or sentiments. To preserve the highest, noblest ideas, we have to tolerate some of the lowest and ignoble. Jefferson didn't like vulgar language or hateful ideas, but he believed that with imperfect people, they are unavoidable. And to try to suppress or censor bad speech puts power in the hands of the government that would cause worse problems (censorship, oppression, and untruth) than the offensive speech. He was always wary of human motives, especially when they were to "help" or "protect" others using the power of the state. And Jefferson had plenty of personal experience with the press's excesses, but maintained that "liberty of all" was the best remedy for falsehood in the press.

Federalist newspapers frequently wrote that he was an "infidel." In September 1800, right before the presidential election between Jefferson and John Adams, the *Gazette of the United States* wrote: "THE GRAND QUESTION STATED. At the present solemn moment the only question to be asked by every American is 'Shall I continue in allegiance to God—and a religious president or impiously declare for Jefferson and no God?'" Other Federalist newspapers printed false articles that Jefferson as vice president was about to resign, that he was "mortally ill," that he had seduced a friend's wife, and that he kept a black mistress.

Jefferson preferred the balanced, responsible journalism of Britain's *Leyden Gazette*—a sober, dignified, and objective newspaper. But most British papers he found biased and corrupt. Often they were simply paid party organs. The British government spent five thousand pounds a year in the late 1700s subsidizing the press. It was consequently viewed with skepticism as liable to half-truths and slanted views. Dishonest. Unreliable.

Jefferson preferred the press to be free and impartial—genuinely and fairly informing the electorate. But when he found in Washington a press dominated by Federalist distortions, he encouraged a countervailing Democratic-Republican press. In 1791 he encouraged a supporter named Phillip Freneau to start the *National Gazette* to counterbalance the Federalist rags. Other Republican newspapers included the *Philadelphia General Advertiser* (or *Aurora*), the *Boston Independent Chronicle,* the *New York Argus,* the *Baltimore American,* and the *Richmond Examiner*. He advocated full and free speech when he urged friends to write letters and articles to counter Federalist misrepresentations, telling James Madison: "Every man must lay his purse and his pen under contribution . . . let me pray and beseech you to set apart a certain portion of every post day to write what may be proper for the public."

When Jefferson assumed the presidency in 1801, he came under continual and vicious attack by the opposition press. An Englishman traveling through the United States during Jefferson's presidency remarked that the terms "Federalist" and "Anti-Federalist" were becoming obsolete. Common terms for the former were now "tories, damned tories, traitors, and British tories"; for the latter, "jacobins, French tories, republicans and democrats" (the last two being particular terms of derision). Pro-business Federalists (like today's pro-business, Religious Right conservative Republicans) referred to the Jeffersonians as "atheists, infidels, drunkards, anarchists, libertines, deists, sniveling fanatics, reptiles, desperadoes, yelpers of the Democratic kennels, tools of a baboon, frog-eating, blood-drinking Cannibals, gallican traitors, demons of sedition, slave-driving nabobs and scum of the political pot." Yet Jefferson always defended the principle of free expression. "No government," he wrote, "ought to be without censors; and where the press is free, no one ever will. If virtuous, it need not fear the fair operation of attack and defense. Nature has given to man no other means of sifting out the truth, either in religion, law or politics. I think it is as honorable to the government neither to know, nor notice, its sycophants or censors, as it would be undignified and criminal to pamper the former and persecute the latter." When John Jay was unfairly attacked in the press, Jefferson wrote, "It is an evil for which there is no remedy. Our liberty depends on the freedom of the press, and that cannot be limited without being lost."

Of course, this meant for Jefferson even the most vicious *political* attacks, such as a journalist who described him as "a man who is a deist by profession, a philosopher by trade, and a Frenchman in politics and morality . . . at the head of a prostituted party . . . I am resolved never to become their property. I do not wish my family vault to be in the guts of cannibals." Of such scurrilous journalism, he states in his second inaugural address:

> The artillery of the press has been levelled at us, charged with whatsoever its licentiousness could devise or dare. These abuses of an institution so important to freedom and science, are deeply to be regretted, inasmuch as they tend to lessen its usefulness, and to sap its safety . . . [but] truth and reason have maintained their ground against false opinion in league with false facts, the press, confined to truth, needs no other

restraint; the public judgement will correct false reasoning and opinions, on a full hearing of all parties; and no other definite line can be drawn between inestimable liberty of the press and its demoralizing licentiousness.

However, when Federalist newspapers would not confine their criticism to political matters, but stooped to printing malicious lies about Jefferson's personal life and character, he advised at the *state* level some prosecutions for libel. This, he wrote in 1803, "would have a wholesome effect on restoring the integrity of the presses." In such a state libel suit, truth would be a defense, but knowingly printing falsehoods would be punished. Jefferson resorted to such a limit on the press when it became so irresponsible that "nothing can now be believed which is seen in a newspaper. Truth itself becomes suspicious by being put into that polluted vehicle . . . I deplore the putrid state into which our newspapers have passed, and the malignity, the vulgarity, and the mendacious spirit of those who write for them." And he'd never even seen the *National Enquirer*! Disgusted with the low quality of most American journalism, Jefferson wrote, "The man who never looks into a newspaper is better informed than he who reads them; inasmuch as he who knows nothing is nearer to the truth than he whose mind is filled with falsehoods and errors."

In spite of his criticism of the lack of quality in American journalism, Jefferson did not deviate from his belief in the freedom of the press: "were it left to me to decide whether we should have a government without newspapers or newspapers without a government, I should not hesitate a moment to prefer the latter." The remedy for biased reporting was not repression and censorship, but increased information. "To punish these errors too severely would be to suppress the only safeguard of the public liberty," he wrote. The solution to a liberal bias in the established media is not firing Dan Rather, but starting new cable networks (CNN).

Similarly, Jefferson expected the federal government (especially the presidency) to be open and honest in its press releases, and he countenanced "leaks" to newspapers if the executive was not complete in its disclosure of official policy. When in 1795 the Jay Treaty was ratified, President Washington kept it secret and the Senate enjoined members not to divulge the exact text of the treaty. An abstract of the Jay Treaty was leaked to the *Aurora* by Senator Mason of Virginia and printed. Jefferson praised this disclosure as a "bold act of duty."

The only limit to government disclosure of official news was, for Jefferson, genuine national security matters, such as military secrets or strategies. As he wrote to Madison in 1789, "the people shall not be deprived or abridged of their right to speak or write or otherwise to publish anything but false facts affecting injuriously the life, liberty, property, or reputation of others or affecting the peace of the confederacy with foreign nations." Even in those cases the government should not have the power of "prior restraint" (censorship), but newspapers should merely be "liable to legal prosecution for false facts printed and published" or security breached.

Still, when president, Jefferson refused to disclose some public documents relating to the Aaron Burr trial. The Congress asked Jefferson to provide information on the Burr Rebellion except "as he may deem the public welfare to require not to be disclosed." Jefferson deemed all the materials in his possession inappropriate to provide, since it had not been given under oath. This was a classic case of invoking "executive privilege," which President Richard Nixon later invoked as precedent during the Watergate hearings, and Bill and Hillary Clinton probably wished they could have gotten away with during the Whitewater and DNC fund-raising hearings!

When the Supreme Court, under Federalist Chief Justice John Marshall, requested documents relevant to the Burr case *and* demanded President Jefferson's appearance as a witness in the case, T. J. offered some papers but refused personal attendance as violating the separation of powers. "The respect mutually due between constituted authorities," he wrote, prevented any branch from calling another on the carpet. The executive must be the sole judge of what may be safely divulged in answer to requests by courts, Congress, or the public.

It was such exercise of executive privilege that prompted Jefferson's opponents to dub him "King Thomas the First." They mocked his public "openness" until he was in a position of authority, and then claimed he was as closed as John Adams. And they were correct in suspecting Jefferson's motives in not cooperating with the Burr case investigation. His personal animosity toward this political rival led him to be less than fair and objective in his case.

Still, Jefferson would be against the "politically correct" speech codes that try to sanitize speech of any "hate" or slurs against women, minorities, homosexuals, the handicapped, Native Americans, spotted owls, etc. The universities and organizations that adopted speech codes soon found how an atmosphere of fear, intimidation, and persecution was created. The United States Supreme Court, echoing Jefferson, has in recent years declared such speech codes unconstitutional as violating the First Amendment right to free speech. The speech codes legally punished certain forms of speech deemed "uncivil" or "hate speech" directed at blacks or other minorities; women; gays, lesbians, and bisexuals; religious groups; or left-handed squirrelophiles. So, to say something like "I just think becoming engaged to a lightning bug and living in the trees is kind of weird" could land you in jail, buddy. Or to say that four thousand years of the Judeo-Christian tradition regards worshiping crystals idolatrous might be deemed "hate speech."

Actually, politically correct speech began as an attempt to eliminate offensive, hurtful language and create a more "civil" atmosphere. Some universities and other organizations called their restrictions on free speech "civility codes." Pretty clever. They discouraged (with legal or occupational penalties) words or phrases (like "nigger" for African Americans or "bitch" for women) that deliberately insulted or demeaned others. Who would not agree that such abusive language should be eliminated? The problem, which Jefferson would have predicted, was (1) ugly attitudes cannot be legislated away, only persuaded or converted; (2) the legal penalties themselves would come to be used hatefully—against the groups or individuals the Civility Police didn't like; (3) the defining of hate speech words would become more and more absurd, until a whole new vocabulary had to be created and learned. So a student was no longer "stupid" but "intellectually challenged"; a person was no longer "short" but "vertically challenged." A girl was now a "pre-woman" (or better yet a "pre-womyn"—taking the "man" out). Any term that suggested any inequality or inferiority was sanitized in this neo-Marxist P.C. speech.

An Asian American Journalists Association issued a P.C. lectionary saying that writers should not use the word "industrious" to describe workers or students of the Asian-Pacific realm (or "reserved," "serene," "smiling," or "philosophical") because it plays into Asian American stereotypes.

At the University of Connecticut a sophomore named Nina Wu thought it was funny to put a sign on her dorm room door listing people who would be "shot on sight," including "preppies," "bimbos," "men without chest hair," and "homos." This continued an almost sacred tradition of college students putting humorous or absurd notices on their dormitory doors. The gay community prompted the university to bring charges against Wu for violating the student behavior code which prohibits "posting or advertising publicly offensive, indecent or abusive matter concerning persons . . . and making personal slurs or epithets based on race, sex, ethnic origin, disability, religion or sexual orientation." She was found guilty and ordered to move off campus and forbidden to set foot in any university dorm or cafeteria.

In the name of "civility" this student's First Amendment rights to free expression were violated. But the P.C. Thought Police subordinate freedom of speech to their group's right to be affirmed by all, at the penalty of legal punishment. Law Professor Mary Becker at the University of Chicago Law School defended this P.C. violation of free speech when she was quoted in *U.S. News & World Report* as saying, "The First Amendment does more for men than it does for women by protecting speech that supports patrimony."

The University of Wisconsin, supported by state statute, banned "discriminatory comments" in the form of "name-calling" racial slurs or "jokes." It is ironic that what once were the best colleges (Swarthmore, Smith, Williams, Vassar, etc.) and universities (Harvard, Michigan, Yale, Wisconsin) are now the most ridiculous for their adoption of Politically Correct censorship and thought-policing. Some have banned classic literature (Mark Twain, Shakespeare, Milton) because it contains politically incorrect (racist, religious, sexist) materials. So the most expensive, prestigious American colleges and universities are now teaching the lowest-quality, politically correct material! Only in America.

At a public library in New Jersey the "insensitive" books were "weeded out." A title called *The Negro in America* was thrown out because it didn't use the officially acceptable "black." The librarian insisted she wasn't performing censorship, just trashing books "due to racial, ethnic or sex bias."

At the University of Arizona the Diversity Action Place forbids discrimination on the basis of "age, color, ethnicity, gender, national origin, physical and mental ability, race, religion, sexual orientation, Vietnam-era veteran status, socioeconomic background, or individual style." Diversity specialist Connie Gajewski said, "We didn't want to leave anyone out." Most P.C. categories leave out only one group: white male heterosexuals (because they, as everyone knows, are the "oppressors"). "Diversity" is now the buzzword for such nonsense and dangerous censorship.

Jefferson would see the danger and tyranny of Politically Correct speech. Even where the Supreme Court has declared speech codes unconstitutional, the intimidation remains: people are afraid to express any doubts or criticism of the liberal P.C. agenda. I was on a panel of judges recently to award a distinguished honor to university professors. One of the leading nominees was an African American scholar. A woman judge on the panel rejected him because one of the letters of recommendation described the nominee as a "Renaissance man." No one (including me) dared to call her on this prejudiced attitude.

Throughout our country Americans have been shamed, threatened, intimidated, and bullied into repressing thoughts they've had contrary to the feminist, black, homosexual agendas. This threatens our democracy. It has led many to cheer on the few outspoken extremists, like Rush Limbaugh. This Politically Correct speech code adopted in many universities a few years ago is different from saying or publishing damaging untruths about someone, like the university administrator at Virginia Tech who sued the campus newspaper in the spring of 1996 for printing an article in which she was described as the "Director of Butt-Licking." That, Jefferson would say, was libelous, since that was not her official title.

Some restrictions on free speech came in the form of anti-sexual-harassment policies. In these the victim of a suggestive slur (such as "Hey, wanna have lunch, baby?") may have the perpetrator prosecuted for offensive speech. Since the "victim" gets to define what is offensive, he/she/it/they make it difficult to decide what one should say to anyone, inhibiting conversation considerably. "My, you look nice today" might lose you your job, house, bank account, and land you in a federal penitentiary. The university newspaper at State University of New York, Binghamton, censored the economics department faculty for the sexually harassing remark that a student was "so smart and pretty too." Better just keep the ol' mouth shut. Of course, some people find silence demeaning, offensive, insensitive, and hateful. You might as well just turn yourself in now. Or maybe have a stack of cards printed up that you can hand to everyone you encounter, saying, "What would you like me to say/not say to you?" That way everyone can just tell everyone else what they want them to say to them today. Jefferson would be incredulous. But he wouldn't say so.

Not that Jefferson would appreciate rude talk, pornography, or profane or insulting language. He personally was the most polite speaker—urbane and civilized, careful never to give offense. His hopes for freedom of speech were the cultivation of reasoned intelligence, advancement of knowledge, and elevation of society. Such wise, tolerant debate (like *The MacNeil-Lehrer Newshour* format) would promote sensible, humane policy and the greatest hope for social harmony. Jefferson wrote of the best kind of American journalism: "freedom of the press . . . is the best instrument for enlightening the mind of man, and improving him as a rational, moral, and social being." The *New York Times* is Jeffersonian journalism; the *National Enquirer* is not. But to enjoy the best, according to Jefferson, we have to tolerate the worst: "Error . . ." may be tolerated "where reason is left free to combat it."

The proper remedy for rude, abusive talk in Jefferson's view is not arming some groups with legal weapons to censor and punish certain kinds of speech that they personally find offensive. That's fascism in sheep's clothing. The proper, Jeffersonian response to ugly, vile speech is civilized, persuasive speech. A kind word turnest away wrath. Or, as the Proverb says, "A word fitly spoken is like apples of gold in pictures of silver" (Proverbs 25:11). Jefferson would tell the vulgar speaker that his/her/its rude language degrades the speaker as much as (if not more than) its victim. And his religious views still held that after death each person will have to give an account to God not only for everything he or she has *done* but everything he or she has *thought* and *said*! As the Bible, which Jefferson was so familiar with, says, "every idle word that men shall speak, they shall give an account thereof in the day of judgement."

Gentle rebuke and biblical injunction may seem weak responses to racist, sexist talk, according to the P.C. Police, but for Jefferson they are much less dangerous to our democracy than punitive speech codes that allow the victims to exhibit their own meanness and intolerance. External laws and rules will not do away with offensive language—only an internal transformation in an individual's character will do that. You can't put new wine into old wineskins, as somebody once said.

Like John Stuart Mill, though, Jefferson did not extend freedom of expression to freedom of action. It's one thing to talk about blowing up a federal building, or even to convey instruction on making a bomb over the Internet; it's another thing to actually blow up the building, killing innocent people. Freedom of thought and speech do not mean freedom of action. And, of course, even speech that causes harm (e.g., libel or slander) can be punished in the civil courts. Society rightly regulates obscenity and pornography, protecting children—even on the Internet. But if government censors are allowed to decide what is "harmful" speech, and outlaw it, fallible and self-interested groups will use it to persecute their opponents.

Such was the case in the 1790s with the Federalists' Alien and Sedition Acts, which punished speech critical of the government—it was used against their political opponents, especially Jefferson's party. The Sedition Act, during the Federalist administration of President John Adams, held it appropriate to punish, legally, publications critical of public officials (such as President John Adams!). For saying or printing something critical of a government official, the act provided for a fine not exceeding $2,000 or imprisonment not exceeding two years. The spoken or published criticism of officials had to be defamatory (negative untruth) and permitted truth as a defense, but predominantly Federalist judges would decide what the truth is. For example, if a Republican newspaper printed a commentary that accused President Adams of being a "fat, ignorant monarchist," it could be prosecuted and punished unless it could prove that the president was (a) fat, (b) ignorant, and (c) a monarchist. Might not be so easy to prove all three things. Then it was bankruptcy and jail time. Sorta makes you think twice before you criticize the president, that Sedition Act does. Especially after it's tried on a few Republican newspapers: the Federalists brought actions against seventeen pro-Jefferson newspapers. No Federalist newspapers were indicted. The *Aurora,* the *Boston Independent Chronicle,* the *New York Argus,* and the *Richmond Enquirer,* along with four other Republican papers, were prosecuted in 1799. Two of them ceased publication. Scary.

What would Nixon have done to the *Washington Post* with such power? What would Clinton do to the *Washington Times?* The 1950s McCarthy era persecuted anyone with vaguely "communist" tendencies (e.g., supporters of the New Deal). The liberal Politically Correct speech codes do the same thing in the name of protecting women and minorities from harassment, abusive and hateful speech; they persecute conservatives. This would prove to Jefferson that neither conservatives (1790s Federalists and 1950s McCarthyites) nor liberals (1990s P.C.-ers) are immune to the temptation to use the law to suppress their opponents' right to free speech.

Only those who are really confident in the justice of their cause and the reason of their arguments are comfortable with absolute freedom of discourse. "It is error alone which needs the support of government. Truth can stand by itself," Jefferson noted.

As Jefferson defined academic freedom of speech at the University of Virginia that he founded: "Here, we are not afraid to follow truth wherever it may lead, nor to tolerate any error so long as reason is left free to combat it."

WOMEN

"Women are formed by nature for attentions, not for hard labor. A woman never forgets one of the numerous train of little offices which belong to her. A man forgets often."

—THOMAS JEFFERSON, 1787

Jefferson believed the radical idea that men and women are different. And like the French, he might have said *"Viva la difference!"* Even before Dr. John Gray's popular book *Men Are from Mars, Women Are from Venus,* Jefferson knew that men and women possess different sensibilities, attitudes, and gifts. And those differences aren't bad; they can complement each other and produce a rich harmony, not just a source of conflict. Appreciating the sexes' different temperaments can be a joy, not a burden.

Jefferson's main experience with women was with his wife, Martha, or Patty. A pretty, petite, vivacious young woman, she was known for her accomplishments in the "feminine" talents of music and dance. It was said that their shared love of music was what allowed T. J. to catch her, despite numerous rival suitors. Family recollections portray Patty Jefferson as exquisitely beautiful, tall with a lithe figure, graceful and attractive. She was well educated for her day and a voracious reader. She inherited from her father, a prominent and wealthy lawyer and businessman, methods of industry, especially in the accounting practices necessary to a plantation wife. She was a young widow of twenty-three when Jefferson married her; he was twenty-eight.

The two were married on New Year's Day, 1772. Leaving the wedding party at her father's estate, "the Forest," in the Tidewater region of Virginia, they rode in a carriage toward their honeymoon cottage in the mountains. A light snow fell as they ascended the hills of Piedmont Virginia toward the site of Monticello. The snowfall became so heavy the newlyweds had to abandon the carriage and continue on horseback. By the time they reached the house, the snow was two feet deep, the servants were all in bed, and the couple's bedchambers were dark and cold. But their love warmed the place and they began an unusually contented and happy marriage. It was tragically cut short by Martha's early death ten years later.

In Patty, Jefferson found the multifaceted, loving, accomplished wife of Solomon's Proverbs:

> *Who can find a virtuous wife?*
> *For her worth is far above rubies.*
> *The heart of her husband safely trusts her;*
> *So he will have no lack of gain . . .*
> *All the days of her life*
> *She seeks wool and flax,*
> *and willingly works with her hands.*
> *She is like the merchant ships,*
> *She brings food from afar . . .*
> *She considers a field and buys it;*
> *from her profits she plants a vineyard . . .*
> *She extends her hand to the poor . . .*
> *all her household is clothed with scarlet.*
> *She makes tapestry for herself;*
> *her clothing is fine linen and purple.*

Her husband is known in the gates,
When he sits among the elders of the land . . .
Strength and honor are her clothing.
She shall rejoice in time to come.
She opens her mouth with wisdom,
And her tongue is the law of kindness.

PROVERBS 31:10–26 (NKJV)

Patty Jefferson did all this, managing a large estate and a growing family while her husband, Thomas, was "in the gates" in Williamsburg, Richmond, and Philadelphia, "among the elders" in the Virginia legislature, as governor, and at the Continental Congress composing the Declaration of Independence.

That Proverbial gifted wife suited the Virginia patriarch Jefferson, and she could never be replaced. Still a young, beautiful woman in her early thirties, she died a slow, lingering death after giving life to their sixth child. In her decline into death, Jefferson never left her side—for four agonizing months. A child of theirs later described the scene: "As a nurse no female ever had more tenderness nor anxiety. He nursed my poor mother . . . sitting up with her and administering her medicines . . . For four months that she lingered he was never out of calling; when not at her bedside, he was writing in a small room which opened immediately at the head of her bed."

When his beloved wife died, Jefferson had to be led out of the room "in a state of insensibility," and then he fainted in grief. When he came to, he was ravaged by the pain of mourning. His daughter remembered that he kept to his room for three weeks: "He walked almost incessantly night and day, only lying down occasionally . . . completely exhausted . . . When at last he left his room, he rode out, and from that time he was incessantly on horseback, rambling about the mountain, in the least frequented roads . . . through the woods . . . I was his constant companion—a solitary witness to many bursts of grief . . ." There was fear among his family and friends that Jefferson would go insane from grief or commit suicide to end the agony.

Jefferson, though still a handsome young man in his thirties, never remarried. It was rumored that Patty could not bear the thought of her children being raised by a stepmother and that shortly before her death she exacted a pledge from her husband that he would never remarry. And Jefferson was scrupulous in honoring his pledges. No one could compare to his first, lovely wife. She exemplified the accomplished, devoted woman for him. From her, he made the observation: "Women are formed by nature for attentions [giving attention, care, concern to others] . . . A woman never forgets one of the numerous train of little offices [duties, responsibilities, charges] which belong to her. A man often forgets. . . ." This amazingly contemporary observation on the differences between men and women shows Jefferson again thoughtful and astute. Women, he thought, were more attentive and multi-faceted than men. Men are more single-focused and goal-oriented (and often stubborn and inflexible) than women. Hence, women for Jefferson are more suited to tasks that involve a multitude of attentions, people, and demands (like running a household or plantation). Today this might lead Jefferson to recognize women's places in many activities and careers in society, requiring a concern for detail and people, like travel agents, executive secretaries, literary agents, and many other demanding, multidimensional, people-oriented jobs. And any mother knows more about managing complex organizations (and demanding people) than a corporate executive or president of the United States.

This Jeffersonian insight into female distinctiveness is echoed in *Men Are from Mars, Women Are from Venus* by Dr. John Gray. In it, the author describes the difference between men and women in this way:

> Venusians [women] . . . value love, communication, beauty, and relationships. They spend a lot of time supporting, help-

ing, and nurturing . . . Their sense of self is defined through their feelings and the quality of their relationships. They experience fulfillment through sharing and relating . . . They do not wear uniforms like the Martians [men] . . . they enjoy a different outfit every day . . . To share their personal feelings is much more important than achieving goals . . .

Martians [men] value power, competency, efficiency, and achievement. They are always doing things to prove themselves and develop their power and skills. Their sense of self is defined through their ability to achieve results.

Since men, and male values of power, dominate politics, Jefferson thought women should not be soiled by such "dirty" activities. And since men and women are so different, Jefferson would see advantages to their being separated at times (in single-sex colleges like Wellesley, or the military, like VMI). He also recognized the chemistry of male-female relations, which cannot be ignored, and affects their working together. Unless very carefully assigned according to their talents and prohibited in combat, Jefferson would not relish women in the military. The defense of our country might be compromised if the differences between men and women, and the chemistry between them (especially in confined spaces, like aircraft carriers), are naively ignored.

Jefferson liked women. Especially beautiful, intelligent, talented, vivacious, charming women. Like Abigail Adams. His circle of friends in Paris included many highly accomplished, artistic, well-educated women. And they liked him. Part of Jefferson's appeal to women was his "feminine sensibilities." He was gentle, shy, sensitive, careful of attentions, like the women he admired. Henry Adams described him as possessing a character of "elevation, versatility, breadth, insight, and delicacy . . . His tastes were for that day excessively refined. His instincts were those of a liberal European nobleman . . . He shrank from whatever was rough or coarse, and his yearning for sympathy was almost feminine." Soft-spoken. Sensitive. Caring.

A prominent Washington socialite described her pleasure at meeting Jefferson for the first time: "This man so meek and mild, yet dignified in his manners, with a voice so soft and low, with a countenance so benignant and intelligent . . . put me perfectly at ease and at once unlocked my heart."

Admittedly, Jefferson unlocked more than women's hearts! Before and after his marriage, he may have had affairs with married ladies (see chapter 6, "Family Values") and kept a black mistress. But if these liaisons actually occurred, they were conducted with such notable discretion that it is impossible to conclusively deny or confirm them. Unlike some Democratic presidents, Jefferson didn't employ the state police or the Mafia to procure his trysts, but he probably, like Jimmy Carter, "lusted in his heart."

The formal legal complaint in federal court by Paula Jones against Bill Clinton includes a startlingly graphic description of the president's (then governor of Arkansas) alleged behavior. Even if Jefferson did seduce the young, beautiful mulatto slave Sally Hemings, I doubt that he went about it in quite that way. Jefferson was sensitive, subtle; Clinton, according to Ms. Jones's testimony, was crude and rude. The evidence for Jefferson's liaison with Sally Hemings is inconclusive; she didn't bring a sexual harassment suit against T. J. She also didn't have the benefit of media access, lawyers, or the National Organization for Women. But in 1974 Fawn Brodie shocked the country and enraged the Jefferson scholarly community by publishing a book entitled *Thomas Jefferson: An Intimate History,* alleging that widower T. J., in his early forties, took the teenage slave girl as his mistress.

"Black Sally," as Jefferson's political enemies called her in the scandal sheets they wrote, was actually the half sister of Jefferson's dearly departed wife, sired by T. J.'s father-in-law (with *his* slave mistress!). Life on the ol' plantation sure got complicated sometimes! Anyway, this meant that Sally resembled Jefferson's late wife: tall, slim, and beautiful. The main evidence Brodie gives to prove Jefferson's affair is the testimony of Sally's third son, Madison, who claimed that he and three other children were the offspring of that union. On her deathbed, Sally reportedly informed her children of their parentage, and now a large black community in America claims ancestry to the author of the Declaration of Independence. Besides these testimonies, Fawn Brodie gives other "evidence": that Jefferson frequently uses the term "mulatto" to describe the color of the French countryside in 1790, shortly after commencing the affair with Sally; that Jefferson described himself as an "orangutan" in a letter of the period (an animal, he wrote elsewhere, that was sexually attracted to black women); that he showered expensive gifts and clothes on Sally; and that he freed only her and their slave offspring at his death.

Several Jefferson devotees and scholars have disputed all this evidence and insist that the whole story is a vile Federalist lie designed to discredit Jefferson and his cause.* Brodie portrays the Jefferson-Hemings liaison as a close, beautiful relationship, intellectual and emotional as well as physical, and of long duration. Not a tawdry, exploitative, oppressive, abusive relationship. I find the evidence and counterevidence inconclusive.

Jefferson had the common eighteenth-century gentleman's attitude toward the "fairer sex"—i.e., patronizing and sexist. Women should not work, go into politics, or fight in wars, but be married, have children, and run the home. He criticized Native Americans for having their women do hard manual labor, saying, "This, I believe is the case with every barbarous people . . . force is law. The stronger sex imposes on the weaker. It is civilization alone which replaces women in the enjoyment of their natural equality." With

---

*An interesting twist appears in Annette Gordon-Reed's new book *Thomas Jefferson and Sally Hemings: An American Controversy,* in which it is shown that the slave woman gave birth to six children—always at a time shortly after Jefferson happened to be back at Monticello from his travels.

St. Paul, Jefferson believed that motherhood fulfilled a woman: "she shall be saved in childbearing" (1 Timothy 2:15); it is, he wrote to his daughter, "undoubtedly the keystone of the arch of matrimonial happiness." American women, much more than French women, he is relieved, are aware of the value of *felicitas domestica*: "American women have the good sense to value domestic happiness above all other," he wrote.

Writing to his newly wed daughter, Jefferson advised: "Be you my dear the link of love, union, and peace for the whole family." For the chauvinist Jefferson, women, as the Good Book says, are to be a "helpmate" to their husbands. "The happiness of your life," he wrote his daughter Martha shortly after her marriage, "depends now on the continuing to please a single person." Wives, he wrote, should not themselves engage in "loud political fever," but rather be "contented to soothe and calm the minds of their husbands returning ruffled from political debate." Hillary wouldn't approve; she is known to smooth her husband's brow by throwing furniture at it.

While president, Jefferson had no wife to "soothe" his ruffled mind; his daughter Patsy fulfilled that role, and James Madison's wife, Dolley, substituted for social occasions as the First Lady; if Jefferson had had a wife while president, he would have preferred a calm, domestic Barbara Bush to an activist Hillary Clinton. Hillary Clinton might remind Jefferson of Lilith, the first wife of Adam mentioned in the Jewish Talmud, whose disobedience caused God to remove her from Paradise and replace her with Eve.

Yet Jefferson respected intelligent, independent women. He provided a classical education for his daughters (along with training in the "feminine" virtues of "dancing, drawing and music," enhancing their gracefulness and charm) and valued and respected them as intelligent companions all his life. Female beauty and charm are not contrary to a woman of intelligence and accomplishments, for T. J. But American women achieved this balance better than decadent, pushy European women, who were as different, he said, as "angels to Amazons." The brazen, disgusting quality of many European aristocratic women (like contemporary singer Madonna) really turned him off.

In the end, Jefferson would agree with much of contemporary American feminism—which seeks to *balance* a woman's role as wife and mother with intellectual and social pursuits. A Virginia lady of Jefferson's day and class (like his wife, Martha) was a business manager of the first order—running a complex and extensive household and plantation: ordering provisions, arranging the economy of the whole operation, educating the children and supervising the servants, entertaining numerous guests and dignitaries, all with grace and hospitality, beauty and charm.

A recent social trend among American women seems to confirm Jefferson's view of women as multifaceted, complex creatures, fulfilled in a variety of activities focusing on "attention." An article in the business magazine *Barron's* reveals that young "post-feminist" women in their twenties are leaving careers to return home as full-time homemakers (at least while their children are small). While in 1990, 75 percent of women aged twenty-five to forty-four were in the workplace, by 1994 only 46 percent of women aged twenty-five to thirty-four were working. The explanations for this trend of women moving back to more traditional roles of wife and mother are varied. Some cite the lower interest rates on mortgages, making it easier for couples to live on one income. Others cite the costs of child care, work clothing, lunches, and transportation as reducing the advantages of a woman bringing home a second paycheck. A former nurse said, "My husband and I sat down at the computer and looked at my salary—minus the cost of day care, gasoline and lunch. We realized it wouldn't pay for me to work." This, despite rapid increases in women's salaries, compared to men's, over the past twelve years: from 1979 to 1991 the male-female wage gap narrowed 12 percent; women's median income increased 1.3 percent, while men's median income fell 14.3 percent. Women in the nineties still earned only about 72 percent of equivalent men's salaries, but that was up from 58 percent in 1975.

Other reasons Generation X women have given for returning to the homemaker role are less economic and more "attentions" oriented. One expressed the feelings of many when she said: "We want to be sure we have a strong family unit. My mother worked, my husband's mother worked; we want our child to have more parental guidance at home. I don't want to worry about my child." Another woman reported: "I'm proud that she [her mother] worked—it was a good role model for me. Though I wished she'd been at home when I was very young." Another twenty-something returning-home mom said, "I may go back to work when my daughter's five—but only part-time somewhere close to home, and only if my husband can give up his coaching job so he can be there when she gets home from school." Of course, the main difference in these nineties women staying at home is that they are *choosing* to do so, unlike the forcing of middle-class women into the home in the 1950s. The only regions of America where the *Barron's* study didn't find this trend of women in their twenties returning to home roles were the "Gold Coast" areas of New York City, Los Angeles, and Washington, D.C., where the cost of living is so high, a double-paycheck family is often necessary to maintain a middle-class lifestyle.

But, whatever the reason, economic, social, or psychological, Jefferson would approve of the trend in America to accept and celebrate the differences between men and women.

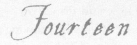

DRUGS

"Infants, maniacs, gamblers, drunkards . . . require restrictive measures to save [them] from . . . destroying [their] health . . . morals . . . family, and usefulness to society."

—THOMAS JEFFERSON, 1823

The main drugs in Jefferson's time were tobacco and alcohol. Jefferson produced both on his plantation, but hardly used either of them. He was mainly concerned about the destructive effects of these drugs. He was like a moderate conservative, critical of liberal "dabbling" in "recreational" drugs, but tolerating alcohol "in moderation."

Although he found viniculture "the parent of misery," Jefferson drank light wines all his life. In France he developed this habit, once ordering 250 bottles of vintage sauternes for his ambassador's residence in Paris. As president, Jefferson spent large sums of money on wine for his dinner table ($2,400 per annum—half his salary!), but he abandoned the tedious European custom of many people standing up and giving toasts at dinner parties, which greatly advanced guests' drunkenness. A visitor wrote, "You drink as you please and converse at your ease." Unlike his rival, Alexander Hamilton, Jefferson was never reported to be drunk in public. He believed that hard liquor had a "loathsome and fatal effect" on human behavior and health. He would drink two or three glasses of wine with dinner "but halve its effects by drinking the weak wines only." He insisted that "the ardent [fortified] wines I cannot drink, nor do I use ardent spirits [whiskey, gin, vodka] in any form." He also did not smoke, chew, or sniff tobacco, a plant he called "wretched."

Although Virginia produced much of the tobacco in colonial America, Jefferson called it "a culture productive of infinite wretchedness." He wouldn't have appreciated spitting in public.

And Jefferson would not agree with North Carolina Senator Jesse Helms and the tobacco lobby that encouragement of tobacco growing is healthy for America. Although Jefferson grew and sold this popular Virginia cash crop, he tried continually to replace it with plants (like wheat) that depleted the soil less, required less work in cultivation, and produced safer, more healthful produce. Of tobacco growers, Jefferson wrote, "Those employed in it are in a continual state of exertion beyond the power of human nature to support. Little food of any kind is raised by them; so that the men and animals on these farms are badly fed, and the earth is rapidly impoverished."

Alcoholism was a major problem in America in the early 1800s, with Americans consuming an average of five gallons of hard liquor per person per year—nearly three times today's rate and higher than any European country, even France! The number of distilleries exploded in America; in the small town of Peacham, Vermont, there were thirty of them. George Washington, who himself ran a distillery, commented in 1789 that hard liquor will be "the ruin of half the workmen in this country." In 1815 a temperance society in Delaware stated that "we are actually threatened with becoming a nation of drunkards." This fueled the movement toward temperance and Prohibition.

Jefferson despised the "loathsome and fatal effects of whisky, destroying the fortunes, the bodies, the minds and the morals of our citizens." He would have similar views on the destructive effects of contemporary drugs: marijuana, cocaine, heroine, crack, etc. Jefferson would oppose any legalizing of these drugs or lessening of the penalties for their use or distribution. He would think these drugs corrode our morals and our democracy.

Jefferson would not be surprised at the destruction contemporary use of alcohol and drugs has brought to America. And he would endorse "restrictive measures to save [addicts] from . . . destroying [their] health . . . morals . . . family, and usefulness to society." He would agree with James O. Wilson, who wrote in a recent article in the *New Republic* that "drugs ravage human character . . . heroin, cocaine and crack . . . lead many users to devote their lives to seeking pleasure or oblivion . . . regardless of the cost in ordinary human virtues, such as temperance, duty and sympathy. The dignity, autonomy, and productivity of users is at best impaired, at worst destroyed." Reports abound of individuals enslaved to these drugs selling themselves, or their children, into prostitution; lying to friends; stealing from family; doing anything to get more of the drug. To feed their addiction. They are in bondage to the substance.

Wilson observes that some people, especially libertarians like William F. Buckley, Jr., think individuals should be free to use any drug without legal restrictions—to legalize all drugs. Most Americans, however, like Jefferson, still believe that society has a duty to protect citizens from dangerous substances, especially cruelly deceptive ones, and to instill in everyone certain basic values, like work, responsibility, family, and decency. Even President Clinton, whose private life has not always exhibited exemplary virtue, advocates personal responsibility and rejects legalization of addictive drugs.

The history of civilizations in decline (such as Rome or ancient Israel) usually reveals a rise in drug use, sexual immorality, idolatry, violence, and other excesses. "Sorcery," which is condemned in the Bible, is taken from the Greek word *pharmakeia*, referring to hallucinogenic drug use in pagan religious rituals. Satanic cults in

America—which combine drug use, sexual perversion, and ritualistic violence—have a long history in deviant Western culture.

The libertarian argument that individuals should be free to do anything as long as they do not hurt anyone but themselves is belied by illicit drugs, as people using cocaine, crack, or even alcohol are less healthy (costing taxpayer-supported health care), less productive (costing national economic growth), less effective parents and neighbors (costing public welfare and police services), less attentive students (costing more in education), and less safe drivers (costing lives). The babies of drug-dependent mothers suffer in health. American society pays the bills for the destruction left by individuals' "freedom" of drug use. Much crime is due to drug addicts stealing to support their habits.

An article in the *New York Times* showed the devastating effects of a highly addictive drug on a small midwestern town. Newton, Iowa, was, until recently, a peaceful community surrounded by cornfields in the wholesome Midwest. The only sounds heard through this small town were church bells, and the jailhouse stayed three-quarters empty most of the time. Kind of a Mayberry of the farm belt. Now the sounds of police and ambulance sirens cut the air, and the town jail is overflowing. The reason for the change? The influx of a drug called methamphetamine, or "crank." It is a stimulant that costs less than cocaine, lasts longer, and gives users a feeling of euphoria and superhuman energy for up to three or four days. Then they plunge into deep depression and paranoia. Terrible crime follows. A man with a spotless record suddenly pulled a string of burglaries; another fled his workplace to get a gun because he envisioned helicopters attacking him; several parents neglected their children so badly that social services took them away; motorists stopped by police attacked police with psychotic tirades. A kind of madness or demonic possession seemed to descend on this little town. The county prosecutor remarked, "Meth seems to have taken control of these people; it's scary stuff." Over time, this drug damages the brain. The schizophrenic behavior produced by the drug (unusual highs and lows) can become permanent, producing insanity. A man in New Mexico beheaded his fourteen-year-old son while high on crank and then tossed the severed head out his van window into busy highway traffic. The drug also causes body sores that reportedly itch like bugs crawling all over the body. Such a horrifying substance, disguised as a drug that makes its users feel happy, Jefferson would want outlawed as a vicious criminal.

But dangerous, addictive drugs are only the most extreme example of this underlying problem of addiction in America. By identifying "maniacs, drunkards and gamblers" as requiring restrictive laws, Jefferson is saying that all kinds of unhealthy addictive behaviors must be addressed by society. People in America are addicted to gambling (through *state* lotteries), pornography (including on the Internet), sexual perversion, and violence. All of these, for Jefferson, would be a sign of an unhealthy society. Dr. Edward Khantzian of Cambridge Hospital found that most addicts are drawn to drugs or other obsessive behavior because they offer a brief alleviation of emotional pain (from the abuse of dysfunctional families, rejection, etc.). The key to curing such addictions seems to be establishing healthier means to healing that pain: therapeutic, community, or spiritual. Alcoholics Anonymous's twelve-step approach of spiritual solace and compassionate community replicates the emotional support of stable, loving families, caring neighborhoods, and dedicated churches that many Americans have lost. For Jefferson, then, the restoration of those older sources of comfort would be the key to solving the drug problem in America.

MANNERS

"In truth, politeness is artificial good humor . . . It is the practice of sacrificing to those whom we meet in society, all the little conveniences and preferences which will gratify them . . . it is giving a pleasing and flattering turn to our expressions, which will conciliate others, and make them pleased with us as well as themselves. How cheap a price for the good will of another!"

—THOMAS JEFFERSON, 1808

American society is becoming increasingly rude. Television programs, advertisements, and movies show more and more vulgar language, insults, humor based on humiliation, and verbal abuse. A recent article in the *New York Times* about salesclerks' behavior was entitled "Service with Some Bile." A neat summary of the decline in American civility was provided by Wayne Barrett of *USA Today*: "American society has broken down, triggered by discourtesy, vulgarity, malaise, toughness, off-color entertainment, a lack of civility and decorum, and a penchant for sensationalism." Dr. Richard Mouw, an ethics professor at Fuller Theological Seminary, recently said, "There is an increasing rudeness in public places"; Americans seems to "take a perverse delight" in harsh, insulting behavior. The "Age of Irreverence" has arrived.

The entertainment and advertising industries promote this trend, using the shocking to get attention and sales. Many celebrities have practically "sold their souls to the devil" by displaying the crudest humor and obscene conduct. Madonna and Michael Jackson parade perversity to millions of impressionable young people, sing lyrics with anti-Semitic, sadistic, and antichurch themes. Children's television has gone from *Leave It to Beaver* to *Beavis and Butthead* in thirty short years. Each generation of Americans gets a little more worn down by public vulgarity, until now it is the norm, almost immune from shock value. Even the profound *Titanic* had to include gratuitous swearing and sex scenes.

The presidency sets the standard for national conduct, and the last thirty years has been a string of scandals, deceit, humiliation, and farce. But President Bill Clinton's reelection amid private and public disgrace was the real turning point of American acceptance of low life in the White House. Low life in high places.

The rise of violent crime in the United States is symptomatic of this overall social collapse in ethical conduct. Chuck Colson, leader of Prison Fellowship Ministries, notes a dramatic change in the *quality* as well as quantity of criminals in America: "The kids I see today—and that's what they are, eighteen- and nineteen-year-olds—are no resemblance to those I saw twenty years ago. Today, if you talk about right and wrong, they stare at you with a blank expression. They're angry, surly, remorseless. Because of irreverence—that loss of respect for transcendent values and for God—we have destroyed the capacity to cultivate conscience and have a generation without conscience." Ralph Reed, former director of the Christian Coalition, explains it this way: "The problem today is that our central institution, the family, is in a state of crisis. One of two marriages end in divorce; one of three children are born out of wedlock; there are epidemic rates of child abuse. It used to be that no matter how tough times got, the family somehow managed to hang on and stick together. Now that isn't so anymore."

Instead of facing our personal responsibility for the breakdown of civility, most Americans make excuses and blame others: temporary insanity, the overall culture, unfair society, or the privileged. Yet, ironically, in a recent *Parents* magazine survey, 82 percent listed tolerance and respect as the most important values children should be taught (75 percent mentioned good manners). Carin Rubenstein, echoing Jefferson's sentiments, writes, "In the ongoing war against rudeness, parents must learn to fight nastiness with kindness, obnoxiousness with respect."

The apostle James wrote that "the tongue is a fire, a world of evil among the parts of the body, it corrupts the whole person, sets the whole course of his life on fire, and is itself set on fire by hell." Words hurt. Insults sting. And multiply. Until the whole society is less civil, less pleasant, less humane. Bart Simpson is funny until we see third graders imitating his vulgar talk and debasing themselves and their friends. Jefferson would be shocked. And saddened. Although vulgarity, insults, and profanity have always existed in society—including colonial Virginia society—they were not, in Jefferson's time, the common or accepted usage. Children had their mouths washed out with soap for cursing; they didn't receive Academy Awards for it. America in Jefferson's time and throughout our history—until about thirty-five years ago (the sixties)—was a more civil, more gentle, more polite society. To some extent that kindness is making a comeback. *Barney* teaches children manners the way *Sesame Street* taught them Political Correctness. Private schools and home schooling emphasize traditional values and manners lost in the public schools. Family entertainment like the movie *Babe* are more popular and acclaimed than horror films with violence and profanity. Jefferson would be encouraged.

As the sixties baby boomers (who ushered in the Vulgar Era) have young children, they don't want *them* exposed to nasty propaganda! "Values" became the byword of the late eighties and early nineties, and foremost of these values were decency, respect, and order. Jefferson would approve. What we need is less "critical thinking" and more reverent thinking. Of course, this pendulum-swinging between rebellion and order, disrespect and reverence, is a constant theme throughout American history. The conformist fifties gives rise to the destructive sixties leads to the Reagan eighties.

In his personal relations, Jefferson was the consummate gentleman: courteous, gracious, and urbane. Henry Adams wrote of Jefferson: "His character could not be denied elevation, versatility, breadth, insight, and delicacy . . . His tastes were for that day excessively refined. His instincts were those of a liberal European nobleman . . ."

That was the impression Jefferson made on almost all who met him. One visitor to Monticello from Boston remarked on "the ease and graciousness in his manners." An Englishman commented on "the most gentlemanly and philosophical" manner of Jefferson. A Frenchman reminisced about his visit to Jefferson's home:

> Let me describe to you a man, not yet forty, tall, with a mild and pleasing countenance, but whose mind and understanding are ample . . . An American, who without ever having quitted his own country, is at once a musician, skilled in drawing, a geometrician, an astronomer, a natural philosopher, legislator, and statesman . . . [with] a mild and amiable wife, charming children, of whose education he himself takes charge . . .

Thomas Jefferson's grandson told many stories of the "polished manners" of this "well-bred gentleman: courteous and considerate to all persons." As noted earlier, Jefferson once chastised his grandson for refusing to return the courteous bow of a black man. On another occasion, as president, Jefferson was riding back to Monticello on his favorite horse, accompanied by dinner guests. On reaching a stream, a poor man asked if he would carry him across on his horse. Jefferson did. Afterward, a guest asked the man why he'd asked Jefferson. The poor man replied, "From [the others'] looks, I did not like to ask them; the old gentleman looked as if he would do it, and so I asked him." The kindness of Jefferson's face encouraged the poor man to ask him for a favor. He was surprised to learn that he'd just ridden behind the president of the United States!

One of Jefferson's "prudential rules" of social life was to "never enter into dispute or argument with another." He claimed that he never saw an instance of two disputants convincing each other by argument, but he had often seen them "on their getting warm, becoming rude, and shooting one another." Rather than arguing with others, Jefferson advised "asking questions, as if for information or suggesting doubts." But "never contradict anybody." That is why so many found him to be such an amiable companion and a good conversationalist.

Still, in politics, Jefferson admired the French aristocrats who started the Revolution of 1789 for their "coolness and candor of argument . . . logical reasoning and chaste eloquence," but he had harsh things to say about his political opponents, calling Hamilton "bewitched," "perverted," "sneaking," and "corrupt." He said that Aaron Burr was "a crooked gun" (is that like a "loose cannon"?) and a "perverted machine." Patrick Henry was "lazy," and the Federalists were a "reign of witches" infected with "madness," "terrorism," and "aggressive usurpations." So, contemporary mudslinging political campaigns wouldn't surprise or shock Jefferson. What would shock and disappoint Jefferson would be national leaders displaying rudeness and violence in their *private* lives: presidents or senators being rude to servants, yelling at colleagues in fits of anger, husbands and wives throwing furniture and curses at each other. Now, if someone hasn't enough self-control to avoid such disgraceful behavior in private life, Jefferson would think, he ought not to be trusted with a nation's affairs: one's private conduct is the true test of one's public character. American opinion polls showing high approval for Clinton's "public" performance while disapproving of his "private" moral standards would be an ominous sign for Jefferson.

President Bill Clinton, unfortunately, fails precisely in this Jeffersonian test of private conduct, personal manners, and self-restraint. His close adviser Dick Morris told the prostitute he frequented that the President's nickname was "the Monster" for the fits of rage he is prone to. These "purple rages" or fits of anger include cursing his closest friends and associates, belittling his advisers, degrading women, questionable relations with White House interns and insulting his wife. The husband and wife brawls between Bill and Hillary are legendary, including one report that a Secret Service man had to intervene to stop Hillary from throwing any more furniture at her husband, the president, because it potentially endangered his life. Clinton's nickname by his favorite intern was "The Creep."

A society reflects the example set by its leaders. A nation led by a president who yells, "Who the hell could make such a dumb fucking mistake?" when an error was made in a campaign schedule can expect to be generally vulgar, crude, and unkind. Or, if it makes light of such madness while continuing to consider itself righteous, it can expect to become hypocritical. Jefferson believed the truest test of our righteousness was the civility and humaneness shown to those closest to us: our family members, coworkers, friends, and associates. It is no use caring abstractly about children if we neglect and abuse our own; it is false to care generally about "the poor" when the needy right around us are objects of our contempt. To proclaim goodness while having adulterous affairs. Jefferson was more apt to do just the opposite: display little acts of kindness, unknown to the public, to his servants or grandchildren, while ignoring them in the abstract. A visitor to his office at the White House once found President Jefferson on "all fours" on the floor giving a granddaughter a "horsey ride" on his back. President Jefferson felt a little embarrassed over the episode, but said he knew the visitor would understand. His personal affections for the young ones overrode his personal sense of dignity.

Sixteen

ART AND ARCHITECTURE

"I am but a son of nature, loving what I see and feel, without being able to give a reason, nor caring much whether there be one."

—THOMAS JEFFERSON TO ARTIST MARIA COSWAY

Thomas Jefferson's life was steeped in art and surrounded by beautiful architecture. One art historian wrote that Jefferson "was unique among the nation's founding fathers in the range and intensity of his preoccupation with the arts." And Benjamin Latrobe, a designer of the Capitol in Washington, said that Jefferson "planted the fine arts in America."

Every visitor to his mountain home, Monticello, is impressed by Jefferson's art collection. Foreign and American guests found Monticello walls "hung thick" with paintings, primarily copies of the masters: Raphael's *Transfiguration*, Ruben's *Diogenes in the Market at Athens*, Maratti's *Virgin Mary Weeping on the Death of Jesus*. Sculpture also abounded at his residence, with busts of Washington, Alexander I of Russia, Napoleon, and Alexander Hamilton adorning stands throughout the house.

Jefferson, like Aristotle, regarded the human aesthetic sense for beauty as innate, and like the moral sense, capable of nurturance and development. To develop people's aesthetic sense, they must be exposed to beautiful art, architecture, and nature. The noblest art, therefore, elevated humanity to virtue and moral excellence by portraying scenes of human goodness, worthy of imitation. Jefferson would have regarded pictures depicting the obscene, base, or violent as corrosive of human morals and destructive of democratic civilization. Whether classical, religious, or modern, Jefferson's taste in pictures always reflected a notion of the noble in the human spirit: sacrifice, courage, love. As early as 1771, at age twenty-eight, Jefferson was recommending classic books on art: Webb's *An Inquiry into the Beauties of Painting;* Hogarth's *Analysis of Beauty,* and Burke's *Philosophical Inquiry into the Origin of Our Ideas of the Sublime and Beautiful.*

In 1782 he made a list of paintings he desired to acquire, including *St. Ignatius at Prayer, The Prodigal Son* by Le Soeur, and *Paul Preaching at Athens.*

As minister to France, Jefferson was able to satisfy many of these desires and began collecting paintings for his official residence. Many of these returned with him to Virginia, including *Democritus and Heraclitus, called the laughing and weeping Philosophers; St. Peter Weeping for his Offence;* and *Herodiade Bearing the Head of St. John on a Platter.* Several of Jefferson's personal collection can be seen in Monticello today.

Upon his return to the United States, Jefferson acquired a collection of paintings of explorers and Revolutionary leaders of his country: Columbus, Cortéz, Magellan, and Vespucci, along with Washington, Adams, Franklin, Madison, and Tom Paine. His favorite philosophers—Locke, Newton, and Bacon—had their portraits on his walls.

As president, Jefferson received gifts of art, including watercolors of birds in Virginia, Native American statuary (including one of a kneeling woman which Jefferson described as "the best piece of workmanship I ever saw from their hands"), and landscapes of American scenery. The majority of Jefferson's collection was of religious subjects. Ironically, although he loved his own art collection, he thought such expenditures extravagant for most (humble) Americans and therefore declared it "useless . . . and preposterous for us to make ourselves connoisseurs in those arts." If he lived today to see inexpensive prints of the masters in every Kmart, he would be amused, and amazed.

To visual art might be added Jefferson's love of musical art. He adored the sweet melodies of Baroque and classical music—Mozart, Corelli, Scarlatti, Bach. Harmony, balance, grace. Joyful, uplifting sounds. Elevating. Happiness-bringing. Cheerful. Ordered. Symmetrical as his beloved Greek Revival architecture. A recent study showed that students listening to Mozart performed better on exams, which would not surprise Jefferson.

As in his tastes in architecture, Jefferson preferred the simple and elegant. He despised the gaudy golden picture frames in Europe, remarking on "the tawdry taste prevailing for the gew-gaw gilt frames, these flaring things that injure greatly the effect of the prints." He preferred simple, plain wooden frames that allowed the eye to concentrate on the picture itself. The pride of ornament disgusted him.

Similarly, Jefferson admired the clean, simple, and elegant lines of the neoclassical, Greek Revival architecture he witnessed in France. Of the archetypical Greek Revival Maison Carrée at Nîmes, Jefferson exclaimed, "I gazed whole hours . . . like a lover at his mistress." And this was not the only classical French building he fell in love with. He confessed that he was "violently smitten" with the Hôtel de Salm in Paris, another graceful neoclassical masterpiece of perfect symmetry, delicate columns, simple, clean lines. "I used to go to Tuileries almost daily to look at it," Jefferson confessed. "Sitting on a parapet, and twisting my neck round to see the object of my admiration . . . From Lyons to Nísmes I have been nourished with the remains of Roman Grandeur." And this nourishment in Greek neoclassical architecture Jefferson brought back to America to design the capitol building in Richmond, Virginia, the famous Christ Church in Charlottesville, and the award-winning rotunda of the University of Virginia. All benefited from Jefferson's love of classical architecture and stand as monuments to his rare taste in architectural beauty. Each is a treasure in America.

The clean, white columns and cubic symmetry of the Virginia capitol was, for Jefferson, "the best morsel of ancient architecture," a "simple and sublime" design whose large, tall windows created a "light and airy" effect inside. "The Capitol in the city of Richmond," he wrote, "is the model of the Temples of Athens . . . and of the Maison of Nísmes."

A Frenchman, the Duc de la Rochefoucauld-Liancourt, affirmed Jefferson's choice, calling the Richmond capitol building "beyond comparison the most beautiful, the most noble, and the greatest in all America."

Upon returning from France, Jefferson redesigned his own home, Monticello, to integrate his new knowledge of neoclassical architecture. Columns, domes, and long windows re-created the effect of the Greek buildings. This classical gem on top of a green mountain above Charlottesville "shines alone in this secluded spot," as the Marquis de Chastellux remarked; and it still draws over half a million visitors every year to its classical beauty and inventiveness. The Duc de la Rochefoucauld described Jefferson's home this way:

> The house stands on the summit of a mountain and the tastes and arts of Europe have been consulted in the formation of the plan . . . the apartments . . . large and convenient; the decoration . . . simple, but regular and elegant . . . infinitely superior to all other houses in America, in point of taste and convenience . . . his house will certainly deserve to be ranked with the most pleasant mansions in France and England.

Not bad.

Late in his life, Jefferson designed the crowning touch of his architectural genius: the buildings on "the Lawn" of the University of Virginia—the most unique academic campus in America. Modeled on the Château de Marly, which was built for Louis XIV near Versailles, Jefferson's design for the university had a massive rotunda as its focal point, with five pavilions on either side of a rectangular lawn. A vision of perfect symmetry and balance, elegant and clean lines, captivatingly beautiful. "Now what we wish is that these pavilions . . . shall be models of taste and good architecture," he wrote. "An academical village rather than of one large building." Not the heavy stone piles of northern universities, but light, elegant, cheerful white columns and red brick. And the classical structure "arranged around an open square of grass or trees." A piece of art to live in. And study in. An aesthetic environment, for Jefferson, contributed to learning. The central, domed rotunda, "its light and airy rooms, white woodwork against white plaster, are among the most beautiful spaces ever created in America," according to Frederick Nichols. "Designed to have ceilings illuminated with stars, to extend the symbolism of the dome as the canopy of heaven."

The Jeffersonian buildings at the University of Virginia still captivate the thousands of visitors a year that come to admire them in Charlottesville; and students compete vigorously for the honor of living in the original student quarters on the Lawn, even though they have to tote their own firewood. A physical and architectural environment suited to enlightened learning, the joyous, disciplined search for truth.

All of these masterpieces made Thomas Jefferson the first great native-born architect in America. Five hundred of his architectural drawings still survive, from early drawings of Monticello in 1767 to sketches of the university grounds in the 1820s. A lifetime of creativity.

Jefferson learned architecture from observation and from classic texts on Palladian design. In a country that had few buildings of distinction (he called the College and Hospital for Lunatics in Williamsburg—he made a distinction between the two—"rude, misshapen piles which . . . would be taken for brick kilns" had they not had roofs), Jefferson planted pieces of architectural beauty that to this day command admiration. His simple, elegant taste eschewed the "barbarous ornaments" of the European Baroque and the "wretched" English architecture of rambling stone piles. Beautiful architecture was regular and elegant, and important to the American Republic, for Jefferson. "How is taste in this beautiful art," he asked James Madison, "to be formed in our countrymen unless we avail ourselves of every occasion when public buildings are to be erected, of presenting to them models for this study and imitation?" Art and beautiful architecture were not superfluous in America, they were necessary to a civilized, democratic society!

What would Jefferson think of contemporary "models" of art and architecture in America? In downtown Richmond, Jefferson's classical Virginia capitol building, with its gleaming white walls and graceful symmetry, is surrounded by tall, rectangular modern office buildings. An oasis of taste in a desert of dullness. Square, plain, functional structures of glass and steel that don't so much offend the eye as deaden it. Modern urban architecture in America, with its credo of "form follows function," isn't so much ugly as nondescript, unimpressive, "underwhelming." Dull. Walking through this maze of modern blah in downtown Richmond, one comes upon Jefferson's beautiful capitol building and finds a pearl in a dungheap. Gold in the dross of modern life. I think it is safe to say he'd be disappointed in American architecture. It doesn't inspire. It doesn't reflect the highest, noblest strands of humanity. It isn't art. It doesn't uplift. It's boring.

Jefferson hoped the beauty of our surroundings, including the aesthetics of our architecture, would please our senses, provide comfort to our spirit, and elevate our minds. Modern American architecture deadens. I think it is safe to say that most homes in the United States would not impress Jefferson. They are plain, uninspiring. A few are distinctive (many in his Charlottesville area), but most are unimaginative.

Thanks to the Jefferson Memorial Foundation, Monticello is

preserved and expanded as Jefferson created it, to be viewed and enjoyed by almost a million people a year. Similarly, the University of Virginia has preserved and cherished the classical buildings around the Lawn and expanded newer buildings in the same architectural style and spirit of the original. But most of America has drifted architecturally from Jefferson's vision.

This does not mean, I think, that Jefferson would have wanted or expected Americans to simply copy and replicate his Greek Revival style everywhere. He would have agreed with Ada Louis Huxtable, who in a scathing article in the *New York Review of Books* decried the mindless and "selective fantasy" of the preservationist movement of Colonial Williamsburg, Virginia, and Disneyland. He would have agreed with her assessment that the best in American architecture is an "elegant synthesis of expression and utility that has always defined and enriched the best of the building art." A twentieth-century example of that might be the postmodernist architect Philip Johnson, whose "lipstick" building in New York, spired Republic Bank Center in Houston, and fascinating neo-Gothic Glass House in Connecticut combine classical lines with contemporary utility. Like Jefferson's beloved Maison Carrée, these buildings can be gazed at for hours with delight—they inspire and provoke thought and appreciation. For Jefferson, like the neoclassical designs, they encourage human striving and accomplishment. Most modern architecture, by contrast, discourages and benumbs. Jefferson would have hoped our cities would be architecturally distinctive, like San Francisco, not oppressive, like Los Angeles. But just as he was a minority in caring about the aesthetics of our homes, schools, and public edifices, it is still a minority of buildings in America that evince a beauty and architectural style. Utilitarianism has triumphed and we are poorer for it.

And what about modern art? The nonrepresentational art of the twentieth century claimed to integrate scientific discoveries, psychoanalytic concepts, and existentialist philosophy into painting and sculpture. Contemporary social alienation was portrayed through disjointed art. Dadaists extolled absurdity and incongruity (the more shocking the better); cubists challenged traditional visual forms; surrealists suggested Freudian disintegration and inner conflict. The results were not pleasant. Andy Warhol gained wealth and fame with paintings of large Campbell's soup cans. As Bruce Hinrichs in the *Humanist* wrote, these modern artists "offered a changing perspective—a new slightly off-kilter glimpse of the world of chaos and cosmos." What's that? "*Slightly* off-kilter?" Jefferson would say "*very* off-kilter"! And he wouldn't be amused. Or impressed.

The modern art that claims to clarify and highlight contemporary psychological and social disorder, Jefferson would think is contributing to it. Where modernists see existentialist relativism, Jefferson saw objective standards—in both classical and Judeo-Christian civilizations. If modern art evokes "the lost, lonely nature of modern life," Jefferson would want it to provide some relief, some solace, as traditional art did. Merely reflecting the alienation and misery of the world is hardly a noble act; traditional beauty provided some positive answers to the darkness and cruelties of life. Modern art, which rapidly descended into obscenity, and elevation of the ugly and coarse, contributed to the nastiness of modern life.

Again, it is important to remember that for Jefferson art doesn't just *reflect* life, it is part of life and will always have a positive or negative effect on humanity. Merely portraying the evil and miserable aspects of society without offering hope or light is to perpetuate that misery. But that's because Jefferson had hope for human goodness and advancement; and his philosophical attitude is reflected in his collection of art—largely along classical and religious lines. To give in to the disillusionment and despair of modern art violated Jefferson's whole nature.

Similarly, modern music that elevates crude instincts and violence would seem demonic to Jefferson. While always defending freedom of artistic expression, he would mourn that so much of popular American music (hard rock, rap, Madonna) is crass, vulgar, and obscene. And he would expect such music to poison the minds and spirits of those exposed to it—damaging psyches and social relationships, especially in vulnerable children. Again, music for T. J. was to elevate the human mind and spirit, encourage, delight, and balance the mind. Not darken and destroy it. But the current vulgarity in popular culture would not surprise Jefferson. He saw its coming in the eighteenth century with sensationalist journalism and crass advertising.

To receive the best in human expression, Jefferson believed, we often have to tolerate the worst. To control and censor would produce worse results. Hypocrisy. Oppression. Persecution of the best by the mediocre. The murder of Socrates taught the lesson of social intolerance. So Jefferson would expect some chaff with the wheat in popular culture. At best, it would make for more discerning citizens. But he still would cringe at much of contemporary art, architecture, and music.

Seventeen

THE ENVIRONMENT

"There is not a sprig of grass that shoots uninteresting to me."

—THOMAS JEFFERSON, 1790

Thomas Jefferson might be considered America's first environmentalist, with his love and respect for nature. Yet he balanced an admiration and awe for the natural environment with economic development and recreation in it.

Living in the Blue Ridge Mountain and Piedmont regions of Virginia, Jefferson had a lot to love in nature. The variety and beauty of natural surroundings there are almost unrivaled in the world. The profusion of lush green trees and plants (oak, pine, birch, holly, laurel, rhododendron, azalea, hickory, chestnut), thick colorful foliage covering vast mountains and rolling fields, bright blue sky and pure white clouds, animals and birds of every description (white-tailed deer, wildcat, gray squirrel, muskrat, rabbit, fox, quail, grouse, duck, geese, red cardinals) and winding rivers (James, Rappahannock, Shenandoah) replete with perch, pike, carp, and catfish provide an exceptional taste of nature's beauty and wonder. He called it the Eden of the United States. He boasted that it had the best climate in the country—early, gorgeous light green springs with a profusion of flowered trees (dogwood, cherry, redbud); long colorful autumns, red and gold; snow-covered white hills in winter; and cool summer breezes on his mountaintop above Charlottesville. An observer captured the striking beauty of Jefferson's Virginia in this testimonial:

> On the west [Monticello] commands a view of the Blue Ridge for a hundred and fifty miles and brings under the eye one of the boldest and most beautiful horizons in the world; while on the east, it presents an extent of prospect, bounded only by the spherical form of the earth, in which nature seems to sleep in eternal repose, as if to form one of her finest contrasts with the rude and rolling grandeur of the west. In the wide prospect, and scattered to the north and south, are several detached mountains, which contribute to animate and diversify this enchanting landscape . . . the sublimest of Nature's operations. . .

As Charles Miller's excellent book *Jefferson and Nature* shows, T. J. adored his natural surroundings, declaring that "all my wishes end, where I hope my days will end, at Monticello . . . many scenes of happiness mingle themselves with all the recollections of my native woods and fields . . . an interest and affection in every bud that opens, every breath that blows around me . . . every object in nature invites one into the fields." In those fields Jefferson was active: riding horses, planting crops, walking, hunting. He was not an abstract, romantic ecologist—he participated in "God's Nature" as an active sportsman, landowner, athlete, and agriculturalist. The land partook of the divinity of the Creator of it; to ignore or damage it was a form of blasphemy to him. "Where has nature spread so rich a mantle? Mountains, forests, rocks, rivers! With what majesty do we ride above the storms! How sublime to look down into the workhouse of Nature, to see her clouds, hail, snow, rain, thunder . . . And the glorious sun when rising, as if out of a distant water, just gliding the tops of the mountains, and giving life to all nature!"

For Jefferson God gave the earth to mankind, "to the living," to use, not to worship as a goddess Mother Earth. Jefferson reveled in agricultural experiments, economic advancements with nature, scientific progress mixing man's God-given reason with the Creator's world to produce goods and conveniences to serve human needs. He would have agreed with his contemporary and friend George Logan, who described economics as "that natural order appointed by the Creator of the Universe for the purpose of promoting the happiness of men in united society. This science is supported by the physical order of cultivation, calculated to render the soil the most productive possible."

Jefferson was not against economic development and did not see it conflicting with environmental concerns. A nail manufacturing factory was constructed at Monticello. He introduced plants from Europe (olives and rice), innovated farm and factory machinery, used natural pesticides (bringing in wild turkeys to control plant worms). Jefferson saw the natural world under man's dominion and stewardship.

Jefferson's scientific outlook approached the vast western frontier with precision and purpose. He divided the American West into a mathematical grid pattern, a rationalistic checkerboard that served utility rather than natural boundaries. Jefferson, as a map of the United States shows, wanted the western territory he acquired through the Louisiana Purchase to be made up of regular, rectangular patterns of states, roads, and fields. Similarly, the great Mississippi River was to be an enormous trade artery with rights of navigation open to all. "Our right is built on the law of nature," he wrote, "written on the heart of man . . . the ocean is free to all men, and their rivers to all their inhabitants" for trade and livelihood.

Jefferson initiated the Lewis and Clark expedition to the great uncharted Northwest for both naturalist and economic development purposes. "The object of your mission," he told Captain Meriwether Lewis, "is to explore the Missouri River, and such principal stream of it, as by its source and communication with the waters of the Pacific Ocean, whether the Columbia, Oregon, Colorado or any other river, may offer the most direct and practicable water communication across this continent for the purposes of commerce."

Jefferson did not see a conflict between loving nature and using it for economic development, so he would at once sympathize with much of the current environmental movement and criticize some of it. Contemporary environmentalists would applaud Jefferson's acquisition and maintenance of the Natural Bridge on his Bedford plantation for public use, his concern for ecological management of the land, and his interest in vanishing wildlife species. Ecologists would be shocked, however, by his view of the infinite supply of natural resources and willingness to use them quickly for human economic development. He would rely more on market forces to manage natural resources than specific public policy. Yet the national regulation of land and water of the TVA, with its soil conservation, reforestation, and improvement for small landowners would probably appeal to Jefferson.

He would go along with the early environmental conservationists who advocated wise use of natural resources, but would not understand the later environmentalists who wished to designate vast "wilderness areas" shut off from human habitation and development. His deistical view of a Creator God giving a "created" world to humanity to use, dominate, and enjoy would be surprised at "animal rights" and Mother Earth devotees who placed nature on a level with mankind (or even superior to mankind!). He would appreciate the National Environmental Policy Act of 1969 with its classic environmental statement: "the continuing policy of the Federal Government . . . to create and maintain conditions under which man and nature can exist in productive harmony." But the later Wilderness Act that sets aside vast tracts of land in the public domain where "man is a visitor but does not remain" would puzzle Jefferson. For him the land is to use, inhabit, enjoy—in a careful, thoughtful, respectful way—but not to preserve isolated as an idol or sacred cow. Still, near his death, Jefferson hopefully, reverently, planted trees, "too old . . . for my own gratification, I . . . do it for my posterity."

So Jefferson would not be opposed to governmental environmental policy—so long as it did not excessively interfere with individual liberty and private property. It's all a matter of balance. Those radical ecologists who want to regulate by law every aspect of business and private life by a kind of Divine Environment (Mother Earth syndrome) would look pretty authoritarian to ol' T. J. Tyrants in sheep's clothing. I mean 100-percent cotton.

He would certainly applaud Heinrich Von Lersner, the German environmental agency official, when in a *Scientific American* article he advocated natural (nonpolluting) sources of energy like sunlight, solar power for houses. Jefferson's home was partly heated and lighted by the sun through numerous skylights in the roof. But Jefferson knew the limits of that energy source; he kept scrupulous records of temperatures—outdoors and indoors at Monticello—and sometimes in the winter it was hard to tell the difference. Several days in January and February with all the fireplaces roaring, the temperature *inside* the house was in the thirties. And when Von Lersner states that "manufacturers will have to produce items that ensure, from start to finish, an environmentally compatible cycle . . . a closed cycle economy accelerate[s] as manufacturers are held legally and financially responsible for the ultimate disposability of their products," Jefferson would hear creeping totalitarianism.

People who tell others what they "have to" do and use the central government to enforce their own vision of utopia usually turn out pretty scary, as Nazi Germany and Soviet Russia have shown. And like "Greenees," they usually start by exaggerating some social problem, then running to the rescue with their half-baked solutions (which turn out to be worse than the original problem).

Jefferson was suspicious of extremists of all sorts, doomsday prophets who have illusions of grandeur. When Von Lersner proudly announces that "improvements in transportation should drastically reduce the number of individually owned motor vehicles on the roads of developed nations," Jefferson would say "Whoa there, Heinrich, we here in America like our 'individually owned motor vehicles,' and having them happens to be a natural right of liberty and property!" If Von Lersner had tried to take away T. J.'s favorite carriage, he'd have had a fight on his hands! Recycling horse manure is one thing but keep your hands off my Oldsmobile (Jefferson, who favored fast horses, would probably have an Aurora today).

When Robert Frosch, again in *Scientific American,* announces that "manufacturers of the next century must consider how to design and produce in such a way as to make the control of waste and pollution a part of their enterprise, not just an afterthought," and that this will require controlling all industries centrally, as "viewing industry as an interwoven system of production and consumption" (are you listening, Karl Marx?). Yipps! Again, people who tell us what we "must do" and think that what we need is a "comprehensive revolution" in economics would sound pretty authoritarian to Jefferson. Fanatics can come in a variety of outfits, including green flannel, faux fur, and Leatherette.

However, seeing the environmental pollution of the twentieth century, and its effects on the landscape and human health (in extreme form in the former socialist and communist countries of Russia, China, and Eastern Europe where unsafe nuclear power plants and unregulated toxic waste have destroyed thousands of square miles of land and injured the health of millions of people), Jefferson would undoubtedly agree with the need for environmental legislation, but in moderation and within traditional American liberties. Which is, so far, what we've done. An article in the *New York Times* on environmental policy since the first Earth Day in 1970 showed that "environmental protection has drastically reduced the threat from most forms of pollution." Several types of air and water pollution have been greatly reduced; 43 percent of toxic chemicals used by manufacturers has been eliminated; America's system of advanced industrial economy with domestic environmental protection is considered a model for the world. Yet the *Times* article points out that two of every five Americans still live in areas where the air is unhealthful and 40 percent of America's lakes and rivers are unfit for drinking, swimming, or fishing.

The key for Jefferson would be balance—balancing the public interest in overall clean air, land, and water with individual and business rights and liberty. One problem he would see is extremists on both sides: on the one hand, individual libertarians and laissez-faire businesses who ignore all environmental problems and resist any governmental regulation and, on the other, environmentalists like Vice President Al Gore who exaggerate ecological threats and want to impose totalitarian solutions to those fictional problems.

A backlash against ecological advocates' exaggerated and unscientific claims began in the 1980s, discrediting much of the Green Community. A petition signed by 1,575 leading scientists that claimed mankind's actions will render earth "unable to sustain life" is an example of such Chicken Little conduct. When Gore chimes in with equally apocalyptic visions of future mass extinctions, cataclysmic climate changes, and gaping ozone holes, as reported in *U.S. News & World Report*, Jefferson would have cause for concern. He knew that tyranny can come in many disguises: wolves' clothing, sheep's clothing, or even polyester!

Admittedly, the challenges of foreign trade deficits, economic competition, and falling living standards exacerbate the resistance to expensive environmental regulations, but Gore characterizing honest scientific skepticism about global warming as "unethical" and based on "kooky theories" is irresponsible. Legitimate scientific qualifications of exaggerated environmentalist claims are often withheld because of a "politically correct" speech code that any questioning of ecological excess is harming "the cause." The result has been some recent embarrassing revelations that "scientific" warnings about loss of rain forests, extinction of species, ozone depletion, and global warming are founded on insufficient or selective data and poor reasoning.

For example, the popular media, children's school programs, and environmentalists' propaganda have asserted a massive deforestation of South America. Figures like 40 million acres a year, or a football field a second, have scared the dickens out of everybody. But over half that estimated total came from one Brazilian scientist who used sensors on a U.S. weather satellite to count the number of fires burning in the Amazon in 1988 (and assuming many of them were the result of recently cleared forest). This faulty figure was grabbed up by the Washington, D.C.–based World Resources Institute and then cited by Al Gore to support the Biodiversity Treaty. When two American researchers used twenty overhead photographs of the Amazon region taken by Landsat satellites, they found the actual deforestation was *one-fifth* of the earlier estimate. Such revelations discredit environmentalists' science and leave Gore with egg on his face.

A similar ecological hoax arose from a study by biologist Norman Myers that predicted an increase in the number of animal species becoming extinct from one a year to 1 million by the end of the century. Myers claimed this was a "reasonable working figure." It was widely reported by the pro-environmentalist media sending panic among the American population. Later, Harvard biologist Edward Wilson trimmed this figure to a modest 4,000, 30,000 or 50,000 species becoming extinct each year. Professor Wilson based his prediction on a mathematical equation that relates numbers of species found on an island and generalizing that to reduced forests on continents.

Unfortunately, many factors besides woodlands affect reduction of species, and continents create conditions for animals different from those on islands. Brazilian scientists actually found an *increase* of species of birds and butterflies in a deforested area. Forests and their species seem to have a natural resilience that even man can't destroy. But the politics of self-righteous environmentalists often ignore scientific data; similar embarrassments have been brought about by later scientific evidence on the vanishing ozone layer and the greenhouse effect from global warming. Despite careful investigations showing the earth's temperature rising at less than half the greenhouse harbingers' predictions, Gore said these scientists "willfully put out false, scientific pseudo facts to pollute the public debate . . . some of these so-called scientists . . . get money from industries that profit greatly from the current pattern." When your theories are disproved, try personal attacks on your opponents. Scientist Stephen Schneider said, "there's an equal chance that we're in a natural cooling trend now . . ." Anyone living in the eastern or southwestern United States the past few winters might agree.

Jefferson would believe that it isn't right to fudge the data, no matter how good the cause. Exaggeration discredits the activists and ultimately hurts the environmental cause.

SCICENCE

"Nature intended me for the tranquil pursuits of science by rendering them my supreme delight."

—THOMAS JEFFERSON TO PIERRE-SAMUEL
DU PONT DE NEMOURS, 1809

Thomas Jefferson had a scientific temperament. He was driven by a desire to learn his whole life. His searching mind was both creative and disciplined. An insatiable curiosity, a passion to know and understand, dominated his existence. He loved science. "A mind always employed is always happy," he wrote to his daughter Martha. "This is the true secret, the grand recipe, for felicity." Jefferson's brain was always learning, inquiring, thinking. A servant at Monticello once described Tom actively studying in his library: sitting on the floor, surrounded by opened books, scanning their contexts, going from volume to volume in search of a solution to a philosophical or mathematical problem. What he would do with the World Wide Web!

As Edwin Martin pointed out in his excellent book *Thomas Jefferson: Scientist,* the third president's accomplishments and discoveries were remarkable, especially considering that his life was dominated by public service and he remained only an amateur scientist all his life. His interests ranged from biology to botany to meteorology to archaeology, astronomy, chemistry, geology, pale-ontology, and ethnology. The guy was a walking Natural Science Department! His stature enhanced America's early reputation in the world of science and technology. He associated increased knowledge of the world with people's social and economic progress. "I am for encouraging the progress of science in all its branches," he wrote, because it will enhance "improvement in their minds, their morals, their health, and in those conveniences which con-tribute to the comfort and embellishment of life." And America, for Jefferson, was uniquely suited to scientific advances:

> What a field we have at our doors . . . The Botany of America is far from being exhausted, its Minerology is untouched, and its Natural History or Zoology, totally mistaken and misrep-resented . . . let them [future generations of Americans] spend theirs [their time] in showing that it is the great parent of science and of virtue; and that a nation will be great in both, always in proportion as it is free.

Jefferson advised one young man, his ward Peter Carr, to pursue science, because "the possession of science is, what (next to an honest heart) will above all things render you dear to your friends, and give you fame and promotion in your own country." Scientific progress would establish American greatness, but Jefferson insisted it was the common property of all humankind, so "any discoveries we can make in it will be for the benefit . . . of every other nation." And rational inquiry spreads democracy as well. "Science is more important in a republican than any other government"—the open-ness of free inquiry requires openness and freedom politically, ec-onomically, and religiously, for T. J. "An honest heart being the first blessing" of life, he told a young man, "a knowing head is the second."

Charles Miller in his book *Jefferson and Nature* summarized well the Virginian's lifelong scientific search for knowledge when he wrote: ". . . he indulged in the rich fields of nature all his life . . . he respected facts and was determined to keep an open mind. He weighed competing explanations offered for natural phenomena. He adhered to or developed worthy methods in scientific work. He admired, in varying degrees, scientists in all fields . . . [and was] especially effective in encouraging others to study nature."

When Jefferson retired from public life after serving as governor of Virginia, ambassador to France, secretary of state, vice president, and president of the United States, he wrote his friend Du Pont de Nemours that he felt like "a prisoner released from his chains" because now he could devote all his time to his scientific pursuits. Yet even when devoting his main attention to America's political matters, Jefferson never neglected his scientific interests. As Virginia's governor, during the American Revolutionary War, T. J. continued his scientific investigations into meteorology, geography, and geology. When he was in Paris as American minister, he consulted European scientists and observed the natural attributes of the Old World. When he moved to the Capitol in Philadelphia as vice president, his baggage included prehistoric bones to contribute to the American Philosophical Society, where he enjoyed "philosophical evenings" with Dr. Benjamin Rush. He even chose his lodgings at the John Francis Hotel because of its proximity to both the state-house and the Philosophical Society headquarters. From there, he corresponded with Dr. Caspar Wistar about the discovery of fossils in New York State.

As president, Jefferson was wont to ride his horse out on botanizing expeditions to the surrounding hills and woods around the Potomac River. A female journalist accompanied him on some of these naturalist excursions and wrote that not "a plant from the lowest weed to the loftiest tree escaped his notice . . . he would climb rocks, or wade through swamps to obtain any plant he discovered or desired and seldom returned from these excursions without a variety of specimens." Jefferson wandered around the vegetable markets of Washington, D.C., to inspect fruit and distribute seeds he'd acquired in Europe. In the White House, wid-ower Jefferson kept flowers, plants, books, a pet mockingbird, tools, garden implements, a drafting board, globes, charts, and scientific instruments. A model of a dry dock he'd designed was on display. The East Room was full of his fossil collection. In the garden was a young grizzly bear brought him by Meriwether Lewis from the Northwest expedition. He amassed large amounts of meteorological data from correspondents across the nation and around the world. He mailed minerals, animal skins, birds, and models of his mold-board plow to scientists around the globe. Once, he discussed the disease cowpox "with the intelligence of a physician" with a Dr. Mitchell. The president's dinner guests were once treated to a view-ing of a "Natural History of Parrots" in French, complete with color plates.

Throughout his busy public life, Jefferson pursued scientific truth in all its varieties, with a boy's enthusiasm. He studied dif-ferent theories of the origin of rainbows, the velocity of river cur-rents, ways to distill fresh water from seawater, archaeological excavations, mathematical principles, and city planning. As my friend Ken Thompson at the University of Virginia's Miller Center once told me: "If you don't find Thomas Jefferson interesting, there probably isn't much you will find interesting."

Jefferson strove to find the origin of Native Americans on the continent through linguistic studies. He investigated new methods for determining the heights of mountains (with mathematics and a barometer); measuring atmospheric moisture with a hygrometer; analyzing wind, temperature, rainfall, and climate changes. His op-tical studies involved application of double refraction to the mea-sure of small angles, magnification eclipses, lunar movement, and the earth's latitude and longitude. He wondered about the value of rustless metal for the specula of telescopes; problems of surveying, coinage, weights and measures; methods of overcoming friction; acids' use in engraving; the bleaching of textiles; varnish as a lining for biscuit barrels; the preservation (with fish oil) of bridge pilings;

gunpowder; and the likely causes of Mediterranean tides. While corresponding with Tom Paine about the political situation in Revolutionary France, he discussed the invention of "hydrostatic waist-coats" (life preservers). In Paris himself, T. J. raced to a demonstration of a boat propelled by a screw revolving in air. He visited Monsieur Ranaudin, the inventor of the new instrument for determining true time in musical movements (largo, adagio, etc.). After viewing the Frenchman's first model, Jefferson suggested improvements. In London he visited a new gristmill operated by steam and discussed the concept of machine "horsepower" with the inventor, Matthew Boulton.

Natural history (animals and plants) remained Jefferson's favorite scientific subject, however, probably due to his rural situation in central Virginia and his agricultural pursuits. Touring Revolutionary landmarks in upstate New York and New England in 1791, he wrote letters extolling the natural splendor of the region: sugar maples, pines, "an azalea very different from the nudiflora," honeysuckle, paper birch trees, "an aspen with velvet leaf," downy catkins, and many other species of brilliant color or texture fascinated him.

Planning his park at Monticello, Jefferson envisioned a variety of animal and bird residents, including elk, deer, squirrels, pheasant, guinea hens, and a buffalo. The Marquis de Chastellux, while a guest at Jefferson's home, recorded watching him feed grain from his hand to the twenty deer that grazed on his grounds. An avid ornithologist, Jefferson spoke of his "enchantment" over hearing a nightingale in France, having his pet mockingbird sit on his shoulder and peck food from his lips, and declaring the stork he saw in Frankfurt, Germany, a "miserable, dirty, ill-looking bird." Inside his mansion were displayed on the walls the heads and horns of moose, deer, elk, mountain ram, and buffalo. Also housed were his fossil collection, maps drawn on buffalo hides, the head of a mammoth, minerals, shells, petrifactions, crystallizations (next to a classic painting of *The Repentance of Saint Peter*), Native American war clubs, arrows, peace pipes, spears, moccasins, wampum belts, and cooking utensils. One journalist described it as "no private gentleman in the world [was] in possession of so perfect and complete a scientific, useful and ornamental collection" in his own home. It was obvious no woman lived with him.

Collections of statistics filled Jefferson's bookcase. While a college student he began recording everything he saw or measured, such as the price he paid to see a prize hog and a tiger and, while ambassador to France, the cost of admission to see a "windless plough" (three francs). As secretary of state he visited an exhibition including "a lion 21 months old" and a small seal. Just before publication of the Declaration of Independence, Jefferson took time out to go to a fair and see a monkey. Later, he paid to see an elephant. A carnival he visited featured a dwarf named Caleb Phillips, an alligator, a trained pig, and "a wax figure of the King of Prussia." Did his curiosity know no bounds? And he dutifully recorded everything he saw.

Mr. Jefferson wasted no time, but was always employed in some intellectual endeavor. His overseer said he was "the most industrious person I ever saw in my life." He only twice saw T. J. just sitting still—once when he had a toothache and once with neuralgia. Trapped by illness in his smaller home, Poplar Forest, Jefferson amused himself by mathematically calculating the hours lines of a horizontal dial for the latitude of his place, finding it 37°22′22″. Stranded for three days by heavy rain in an overseer's shack, with only an old almanac to read, Jefferson spent the time computing how long it would take to pay off the national debt! (Today he might have to be stranded for more than three days!)

Carrying a pocket ruler with himself at all times, Jefferson was once seen measuring the trunks of fig trees in Marseilles. No wonder he had little time for romance! Back home at Monticello, he weighed his peas, counted how many strawberries each plant bore, and measured the length of a horse's stride. Is this guy a fanatic, or what? He kept a written schedule of the earliest and latest appearance of thirty-seven vegetables on his farm. He recorded the first sightings (or soundings) of birds, insects, and frogs. In New York he heard the first whippoorwill on June 8. First swallows and martins on April 21. Frogs croaked in Philadelphia earlier in 1791 than 1800 (probably due to the capital being moved to Washington . . .). From his records, Jefferson once predicted that katydids would make their appearance at Monticello sometime between July 14 and July 20. Fireflies lightly shined on the night of May 8. He counted his letters, informing John Adams that in 1820 he received 1,267. He sent General George Washington notes he'd taken on the Canal of Languedoc in southern France, for future reference in planning the canal near the Potomac.

Returning to America from Europe, T. J. brought eighty-six packing cases, fifteen of which contained books. He recorded the number of pages of the books according to subject. Science came in fourth (after history, law, and fine arts).

Jefferson's criterion for ranking the value of different branches of science was "usefulness." He valued most the practical benefits of science—to economic development and human convenience and happiness. That is why he most esteemed botany (for its agricultural benefits), meteorology (for its effects on human life), and biology (for the benefits to human civilization). He was not completely opposed to pure research or abstract speculations, but for a relatively poor, growing nation like the United States, he believed it was a luxury (like expensive art collections) that we could not afford. Yet he admitted that pure science, research pursued purely for its truth value without a tangible benefit in mind, could lead to practical inventions. He once wrote that "no discovery is barren; it always serves as a step to something else." For example, he praised a "charming treatise on manure" saying that it proved that "science never appears so beautiful as when applied to the uses of human life." Jefferson even applied this to the science of ethics, hoping that philosophers would never give up the "morals of Jesus" for the "mysteries of Plato," because, he said, "the doctrines of Jesus are simple and tend all to the happiness of man."

Usefulness was Jefferson's standard. Agriculture was the most useful activity because it provided the most basic need, food, for human beings, and is the foundation on which all other business activities and wealth are based. He wrote to Georgia's Governor Milledge that "the scripture precept of 'prove all things and hold fast that which is good' is peculiarly wise in objects of agriculture." Jefferson was advanced in agricultural experiments in Piedmont Virginia. He did a one-acre experiment in 1795 that showed, contrary to common opinions, that exhausted soil was as capable of growing wheat as it was rye. Crop rotation and contour plowing attracted his notice and experimentation. Jefferson asked permission to try agricultural methods developed by neighboring farmers (such as a new way of planting corn on unplowed land) and gave freely to those neighbors any discoveries he'd made. He led the way in trying new seeds and plants in Virginia. His exhaustive recorded data (in his *Garden Book, Farm Book,* memoranda, and correspondence) reveal that Jefferson tried new upland rice, silk nettle, pecans and walnuts, enormous cabbage breeds (including one that grew seven feet high!), giant cucumbers, French figs, British vetch, European fiorin grass, New York peas, Italian strawberries, capsicum from the southwestern United States, sugar maples, and apricots. He exposed his dinner guests at Monticello to salads made with benne oil instead of olive oil and native Virginia wines, and the favorable responses of his "guinea pigs" led him to advocate the native products' expansion over imported oils and wines. His experimental garden at the University of Virginia proposed "exotics of distinguished usefulness," such as the cedar of Lebanon, mahogany, the Indian rubber tree, and teak.

As a member of the Association of Agricultural Societies, dedicated to progress in farming techniques, Jefferson loved seeing advances in this science. Probably his most famous invention, a new plow or moldboard, was T. J.'s proudest accomplishment. "The offices of the mould-board are to receive the sod after the share has cut under it, to raise it gradually and to reverse it," he wrote. "The fore-end of it, then, should be horizontal to enter under the sod, and the hind end perpendicular to throw it over; the intermediate surface changing gradually from the horizontal to the perpendicular. It should be as wide as the furrow . . ." Using mathematical calculations to draw a design of a plow to turn over the most earth with the least effort, Jefferson then had it constructed out of a single piece of wood.

The result was the most effective plow ever developed in America, which drew attention in England's Board of Agriculture and around the world, and which is also a piece of graceful art as well— a beauty to behold. The synthesis of science, art, and technology! A sculptured piece of wood that could sit on an art museum's stand and a practical implement that increased the efficiency of food production manyfold!

Jefferson was justifiably pleased. "The plow," he wrote, "is to the farmer what the wand is to the sorcerer," and since it produces the most essential commodity to humanity, sustenance itself, the plow is "the most useful of the instruments known to man." Looking at the practical manufacture of this plow, Jefferson declared that one of its greatest advantages was its simplicity of construction, even "by the most bungling carpenter," who could easily carve one and never "vary a hair's breadth in its form, but by gross negligence." Simplicity of manufacture, reliability, ease of repair were cardinal virtues in Jefferson's technological developments. He might have something to say about today's computers!

Other inventions that T. J. either created or supported included the hot air balloon (in which he saw travel and military uses); construction of dry docks for storage of naval vessels; the submarine with torpedoes (for a young U.S. Navy to sink the large British fleet); fireproof house ceilings (using sheet iron); and scientific instruments: telescopes, magnifying glasses, bifocal glasses, camera obscura, carriage odometers, and personal pedometers. His home contained the new dumbwaiters then in vogue in France—allowing the different courses of meals to be served from the kitchen and wines from the cellar to be provided to dinner guests without constant interruptions from servants. A similar contrivance was a turnstyle for hanging up coats and breeches. One visitor lingered over an unusual piece of furniture in Jefferson's study and inquired about it. Jefferson obliged him by touching a spring on the cabinet, causing the doors to fly open, disclosing a goblet of water, a decanter of wine, a plate of cakes, and other objects. The master of Monticello explained that this provided snacks when he sat up late reading and didn't want to disturb sleeping servants.

Jefferson sat in a swivel chair of his own design, wrote on a slanting lap writing desk he invented, walked with a cane he devised containing a seat that folded out of the handle (allowing him to rest while directing the construction of the University of Virginia late in life), and copied his letters with a prehistorical copy machine called a polygraph ("the finest invention of the present age," he said). These, he predicted, would be preserved and celebrated on future Fourth of Julys "as the relics of the saints are in those of the Church." He advanced the decimal system in American coinage and carefully designed a flashy carriage drawn by four horses (the eighteenth-century equivalent of the GM Northstar V-8!) with a convertible leather top "which could be readily arranged to exclude rain or leave the vehicle entirely uncovered." A convertible roadster with a "spare horse" trailing behind.

After the agricultural sciences, and related to them, Jefferson was most interested in meteorology. Oh, how he would have loved the Weather Channel! T. J. was the best-informed eighteenth-century American on the science of weather. While Harvard's John Winthrop, Benjamin Franklin, and Rev. John Campanus of Delaware kept sporadic records of North American weather, Jefferson observed meteorological events and kept weather data all his life. He intermingled it in letters on other subjects. In an epistle to William Short on the new U.S. Constitution, Jefferson opens with recent weather observations. Writing to President James Madison about problems in the War of 1812, he concludes that "we have had three days of excessive heat [at Monticello]. The thermometer on the 16th was 92 degrees, on the 17th, 92 and-a-half degrees, and yesterday at 93 degrees. It has never before exceeded 92 and-a-half degrees at this place [the mountaintop above Charlottesville]; at least within the periods of my observations." Even at the dramatic opening of the American Revolution, in July 1776, Jefferson found time to calmly record that on July 2 at 6:00 A.M. the temperature was seventy-eight degrees. On the fateful day of the proclamation of the Declaration of Independence, July 4, he noted that it was sixty-eight degrees at 6:00 A.M. and seventy-three and a half degrees at 9:00 P.M. A pleasant day for the birth of the country! On July 8 he wrote down that he paid one Mr. Sparhawk four pounds, ten shillings for a barometer (he knew the pressure on the nation was going to be increasing).

On board the ship *Ceres* to France in 1784, Jefferson made temperature readings. Touring southern France in 1787, he made ten morning temperature observations at Nîmes, St. Remis, Aix, and Marseilles, finding an average of fifty-two and a half degrees, forty-six degrees, and sixty-one degrees for the greatest and lowest morning heats. Thinking always of his native homeland, Virginia, he begged his daughters to keep records of temperatures, bird appearances, insect arrivals, and leafing of trees at the plantation surrounding Monticello, and write them to him in their letters.

As with all his scientific knowledge, he loved to share it with others. T. J. became an unofficial weather bureau for many of his correspondents. Volney turned to him for accurate figures on the winters of 1779, 1789, 1793, 1796, and 1797. He informed Dr. Nathaniel Chapman, first president of the American Medical Association, that according to his records while president, from 1802 through 1809 "the average fall of snow . . . was only fourteen and a half inches, and that the ground was covered but sixteen days in each winter on the average of the whole." What a difference two hundred years can make! Or, maybe it was an eighteenth-century El Nino!

At home, from 1776 to 1820, Jefferson took regular temperature readings, both inside and outside the house. These records show that on January 21, 1810, it was 9.75 degrees outside, 21.3 degrees in the greenhouse, and 37 degrees in his bedroom! It's no wonder, there on the top of the mountain, where winter winds howled and even multiple fireplaces failed to keep the house warm, the ink in his fountain pen froze one day while he was writing! Still, Jefferson seemed more suited to the cold than to the humid heat of lowland Virginia summers. He corresponded in 1779 with the president of William and Mary College in the Tidewater region and found that Monticello averaged over six degrees cooler than Williamsburg. This was partly due to Monticello being 52′ 22″ north of Williamsburg, but T. J.'s residential situation, on top of a mountain—with cool breezes all summer—made it one of the coolest, pleasantest places in central Virginia. And to him, this was not inconsequential only to human comfort; he believed the weather and atmospheric conditions directly affected human attitudes and behavior. The northeast winds that predominate in Williamsburg were "loaded with vapor," according to Jefferson, causing "a distressing chill" and producing effects "heavy and oppressive to the spirits"; whereas the northwest winds that predominate in Charlottesville were "dry, cooling, elastic, and animating." This may account for the different academic atmospheres at William and Mary College and the University of Virginia! He didn't mention the wind direction in Richmond, the state capital, but it seems like it was northeastern during Governor Wilder's administration, but has turned northwestern since Governor Allen assumed office.

Jefferson adhered to the common eighteenth-century opinion that the natural surroundings of humans (including weather, foliage, animal life) had a tremendous influence on their health, height, weight, color, beauty, ideas, intellect, and even sexual potency. Winds, temperature, humidity, rainfall, snow, aridity, purity of air, and quality of sunlight all affected human beings deeply. Frenchman Montesquieu had given this, along with much of his political philosophy, to Mr. Jefferson. European scientists of Jefferson's day used this to "explain" the degenerate nature of New World species and people. This Old World snobbery infuriated Jefferson, and he spent years gathering evidence to refute their claims. He sent charts comparing European and North American animal weights to Buffon, the leading French naturalist.

	EUROPE (pounds)	AMERICA (pounds)
Bear	153.7	410
Beaver	18.5	45
Otter	8.9	12
Marten	1.9	6
Flying squirrel	2.2 (oz)	4 (oz)
Cow	765	2500

Later, M. Buffon wrote to Jefferson that his study on *histoire naturelle* would certainly have benefited from the American's scientific information.

A contemporary of Jefferson's applied the "environmental" theory of human behavior to different regions *within* the United States, concluding that northern New Englanders' long, dreary winters explain their bleak, churlish personalities. Warm, southern climates account for the slothful, drunken conduct of its residents. Florida's air is better than the "noxious exhalations" of Georgia. But another observer declared that drunkards in New Hampshire did not die early because the crisp air had the effect of preserving them!

Virginians like Jefferson countered that the Old Dominion's climate was the healthiest in the world. The fact that it was "God's country" was even proved by the Bible, as Virginia is the same latitude as Jerusalem. Its long temperate autumns and springs delighted Jefferson. He suffered greatly whenever he had to live in a colder climate like France, saying, "it is altogether unaccountable how any man can stay in a cold country who can find room in a warm one." Thinking of our northern neighbors, he wrote, "The Canadian glows with delight in his sleigh and snow; the very idea of which gives me the shivers." Jefferson assumed that "no poet can flourish north of the Alps" because "a poet is as much a creature of climate as an orange or palm tree." In old age, T. J. felt the cold even more terribly, telling John Adams that he shuddered at the approach of winter and wished he could curl up and sleep through it "with the dormouse, and only wake with him in Spring . . ."

Unlike America's recent extreme weather and natural disasters (severe winters and snow in the South, earthquakes, floods, and tornadoes), which are approaching apocalyptic proportions, Jefferson found the nineteenth-century climate moderating. "Both heats and colds are become much more moderate within the memory even of the middle-aged," he observed. And Virginia was the best. Trying to lure a Harvard professor to come and teach at the University of Virginia, T. J. assured him that "there is not a healthier or more genial climate in the world."

After botany, biology, and meteorology, Jefferson had mixed feelings about the other branches of science. He defended chemistry as "among the most useful of sciences, and big with future discoveries for the utility and safety of the human race." But he still regarded it mostly as "cookery." To his grandson, Jefferson wrote: "It is the least useful and the least amusing to a country gentleman of all the ordinary branches of science . . . for chemistry you must shut yourself up in your laboratory and neglect the care of your affairs and of your health which calls you out of doors."

Jefferson would loathe being cooped-up inside a laboratory; he enjoyed roaming around the countryside too much.

Of an anthropological book of his day, Jefferson remarked, "He selects . . . all the facts, and adopts all the falsehoods which favor his theory, and very gravely retails such absurdities as zeal for a theory alone could swallow."

Similarly, he showed little interest in or respect for geology. "To [it] I would give the least possible time." Mineralogy was valuable, but scientific attempts to date the formation of the earth or its mode of creation were ridiculous to Jefferson. To try to reconstruct "what the fiat of the Creator would effect by a single act of will, is too idle to be worth a single hour of any man's life." Of course, this is a man who accepted Voltaire's theory that rocks grow!

Jefferson's Scientific Method

Thomas Jefferson was a "deistic scientist." That means that he believed that God (or the Creator, the Maker, or the First Cause or Mover) constructed the world, the whole universe, is outside it, and established all its species and laws in time. So Jefferson would agree with contemporary creationists in rejecting evolution (not because God couldn't arrange creation in that way, but because radical evolution holds that the world and its species develop out of themselves, internally, not out of an external Creator). Yet, like adherents of the modern scientific method, such as Galileo, Descartes, Bacon, and Newton, Jefferson believed that once God created this world and all in it, the best means of studying it was as material data, with sensory perception. Pure reason was the appropriate means for knowing about religion, morals, politics, and philosophy, but nature is best known by scientific observation, analysis, and verification.

In this deistical science, Jefferson is in a long line of thinkers, including Aristotle, St. Thomas Aquinas, Sir Isaac Newton, and John Locke. All assumed a wise, powerful Creator initiating the world and operating it by "self-evident" principles. The Greek philosopher Aristotle conceived of a First Mover creating all things, each with its own *telos*, or purpose, harmoniously growing and relating to other creatures from a fixed, lawful internal order. St. Thomas Aquinas integrated this Aristotelian system with Judeo-Christian theology, making the God of the Bible the Prime Mover who governs the universe through a series of laws: Divine Law, God's perfect eternal law, revealed partially through Scripture and revelation; natural law, governing the created universe with instinct, laws of motion, seasons, planets, etc. (and participated in by humans through reason); and human law, a subset of these, the more relative, changeable social ordinances that ultimately depend on the higher laws.

Sir Isaac Newton, the great modern English scientist who discovered the law of gravity and the particle theory of light, reflected this view when he wrote: "We are to acknowledge one God, infinite, eternal, omnipresent, the Creator of all things, most wise, most just, most good, most holy. We must love him, fear him, honor him, trust in him, pray to him, give him thanks, praise him, hallow his name, obey his commandments . . . and his commandments are not grievous."

The British philosopher John Locke applied natural, God-given law to politics and most influenced Jefferson in the Declaration of Independence. Like William Blackstone, the English jurisprudence scholar whom T. J. read in his legal studies, the tie between the Deity and social law was assumed:

> Man, considered as a creature, must necessarily be subject to the laws of his Creator, for he is entirely a dependent being . . . And, consequently, as man depends absolutely upon his Maker, for everything, it is necessary that he should in all points conform to his Maker's will . . . this will of his Maker is called the law of nature . . . These laws laid down by God are the eternal immutable laws of good and evil . . . it is bind-

ing over all the globe . . . no human laws are of any validity if contrary to this.

So Jefferson's deistical science drew from a long line of great thinkers and saw no essential conflict between religion and science. Jefferson would agree with his friend Dr. Benjamin Rush, who wished "the divine and the philosopher" to "embrace each other," because "in the judgement of the ALL WISE, it ought to be so; we ought to submit reverently to the decision." The relation between the Creator and his creation is discovered "in the fair volumes of Creation around us, and in the fairer volume of his written Word."

Even without the biblical account of creation in the Book of Genesis, Jefferson insisted we would know the truth of it through reason and observation:

> I hold . . . that when we take a view of the universe, in its parts, general or particular, it is impossible for the human mind not to perceive and feel a conviction of design, consummate skill, and indefinite power in every atom of its composition. The movement of the heavenly bodies, so exactly held in their balance . . . the structure of the earth itself, with its distribution of lands, waters, and atmosphere; animal and vegetable bodies, examined in all their minutest particles; insects, mere atoms of life, yet as perfectly organized as man or mammoth; the mineral substances . . . it is impossible, I say, for the human mind not to believe, that there is in all this, design, cause and effect, up to an ultimate cause, a Fabricator of all things from matter and motion, their Preserver and Regulator while permitted to exist in their present forms . . . evident proof of the necessity of a superintending power, to maintain the universe in its course and order . . . So irresistible are these evidences . . . that of the infinite numbers of men who have existed through time, they have believed, in the hypoth-

esis of an eternal pre-existence of a Creator, rather than that of a self-existent universe . . .

This creationist view rejected the evolution or extinction of species: "every race of animals seems to have received from their Maker certain laws of extension at the time of their formation." And, he wrote, "Such is the economy of nature, that no instance can be produced of her having permitted any race of her animals to become extinct" within the great chain of being. When prehistoric mammoth bones were discovered by Dr. Goforth in Big Bone Lick, Kentucky, Jefferson simply assumed that such giant creatures still existed in the far-north woods, and this, he was pleased to say, was confirmed by Indian legends (look out, Bigfoot!). The existence of seashells on top of mountains in South America merely confirmed the biblical account of Noah and the Flood.

That Divine Creator, for Jefferson, is a spirit outside of nature who created the universe, and he could not be known fully by our limited human minds; but through reason and empirical observation we could know something of his material creation, and this is science. Like the ancient Greek materialist Lucretius, a favorite writer among Enlightenment scientists, Jefferson believed that the reality left us by God is made up of "matter in motion," the smallest unit of which is the "atom." Natural science, then, proceeds through human sensory study of the material world, which is tangible, concrete, and observable (even if only with the help of instruments). Scientific truth, therefore, required observable data that was verifiable—that is, could be replicated by other scientists using the same methods of investigation. A realization of the "partial" nature of this material, worldly reality, along with our limited human mental capacities to properly comprehend it, should, for Jefferson, produce a humility before God and God's nature, not an arrogant, proud, Faustian attitude of man controlling it. Hence Jefferson's caution in reaching scientific conclusions without extensive data and evidence supporting them. Speaking of the physical operations of the brain, he said, "The modus operandi of nature in this, as in most other cases, can never be developed and demonstrated to beings as limited as we are."

The discovery of scientific truth is slow and arduous, requiring, for T. J., "a patient pursuit of facts, and cautious combination and comparison of them"; this is just "the drudgery to which man is subjected by his Maker, if he wishes to attain sure knowledge." Consequently, Jefferson saw reality made up of unique particulars—like snowflakes, no two exactly the same—and was a bit suspicious of rigid categories of natural phenomena. Still, for practicality's sake he organized his own library, and those of public schools and the University of Virginia, along Bacon's lines of human knowledge (memory, reason, and imagination). Jefferson's library classification went this way:

   I. History (memory)
         Civil (political and ecclesiastical)
         Natural (physics, animals, vegetables, minerals,
            occupations)

  II. Philosophy (reason)
         Moral
         Mathematical

 III. Fine arts (imagination)
         Literature
         Languages
         Arts, etc.

For public schools:

    Mathematics
      Pure math
      Physiomathematics
      Physics or natural philosophy

Chemistry
  Natural history
  Botany
  Zoology
  Anatomy
  Medicine

University of Virginia professorships (1824):

Natural philosophy
  Mathematics
  Engineering
  Physics
  Astronomy

Natural history
  Botany
  Zoology
  Mineralogy
  Chemistry
  Geology
  Rural economy

These categories of learning created some problems for Jefferson. In 1824 he wrote a letter expressing a desire to develop a "science of the mind" (today's psychology), but he couldn't figure out what category to put it in or what to name it. He finally settled on the title "moral zoology." He hadn't met Freud.

Despite his many skills and accomplishments in science, Jefferson was ridiculed for his interests by political enemies during his lifetime. In nineteenth-century America, as today, there was a certain anti-intellectualism that distrusted the "fuzzy-headed" thinking of intellectuals, academics, and "philosophers" (a la the Nutty Professor). T. J.'s political opponents tapped into this popular resentment to cut Jefferson down to size. They criticized his "philosophical fogs" and ridiculed him, like radical Tom Paine's amusing himself "with impaling butterflies and pickling tadpoles." A sarcastic Fourth of July speech in 1799 entitled "Sun Beams May Be Extracted from Cucumbers" supposedly detailed Jefferson's scientific experiments on how to make "a marble pin cushion," prevent the growth of wool on sheep, abolish the use of words, and extract sunbeams from cucumbers. Such "quackery and nonsense" disqualified Jefferson from serious public service. Others lampooned his interest in American Indians, suggesting a perverse motive in his studies: Jefferson was "examining minutely every part of [the Indian's] frame" and finding that although the Native American's hand is smaller than the European's, *"ses organes de la génération ne sont plus faibles ou plus petits"* (his organs of generation are not feebler or smaller). His many inventions were ridiculed by his enemies, calling his swivel chair a "whirligig" from which he could look in all directions at once; his merino sheep raising was an attempt to "propagate the breed of naked sheep"; he was a feeder of "prairie-dogs and bullfrogs," a weigher of "rats and mice." A mock diary entry had Jefferson writing "a page of my dissertation on cockroaches."

Yet Jefferson's wide-ranging scientific knowledge and investigations gave America an international reputation for invention and discovery in the late eighteenth and early nineteenth centuries, a great service to a New World regarded by Europeans as a savage, backward place. As a sign of this worldwide recognition, Jefferson was elected to several scientific societies, including the Institut de France, the Dutch Royal Institute of Sciences, the Board of Agriculture in London, the Agronomic Society of Bavaria, the Agricultural Society of Paris, the Linnaean Society of Paris.

Contemporary American science seems to be coming closer and closer to Jefferson's general perspective. The old antagonism between science and religion is breaking down. On the volatile subject of evolution, church and academy are growing closer and less hostile. Noted astronomer Robert Jastrow said in the *New York*

Times Magazine that the Big Bang theory of creation confirms the biblical view of the origins of the universe. Pope John Paul II recently announced that scientific theories of evolution may be compatible with Catholic Church doctrine. Meanwhile, the latest archaeological finds suggest that scientific discovery itself is challenging Darwinism. Jefferson would be fascinated with these developments, as well as the rise of computer technology and genetic engineering.

Nearly 150 years after Charles Darwin's theory of evolution changed the way humans saw their origins, Pope John Paul II made the pronouncement that mankind could have been created by God in a gradual, evolutionary way. Still, the pontiff insisted that even if the human body emerged over time, God's creation (or infusing) of the "soul" was immediate. The nuclear physicist Antonino Zichichi responded by saying that "the Holy Father recognizes science as a depository of values that are on the same plane as those of the faith. The third millennium will set the stage for this grand alliance between faith and Galilean science." Msgr. Francis Maniseaico was not quite as enthusiastic, qualifying the pope's pronouncement with: "what belongs to science belongs to science, and what belongs to religion belongs to religion." Religious and scientific truth will ultimately be in harmony, but they rest on different grounds.

Part of the Roman Catholic Church's opposition to evolution was its use by communists to justify atheism. Pope Pius XII in 1950 wrote that Darwinism was "gladly made use of by the proponents of Communism to make of themselves defenders and propagandists of dialectical materialism and to take from minds every notion of God." Unlike Protestant Fundamentalistism, Catholic doctrine now does not take the biblical view of creation or Genesis literally, but rather sees it symbolically, allowing room for scientific knowledge to fill in the gaps. Even the Bible says that to God "a day is as a thousand years," allowing the seven days it took the Lord to make earth some latitude.

At a scientific conference at the University of Wisconsin cele-brating the seventieth anniversary of the Scopes "Monkey Trial," the seeming Jeffersonian truce over evolution was manifest, echo-ing a National Academy of Sciences declaration that "religion and science are separate and mutually exclusive realms of human thought whose presentation in the same context leads to a mis-understanding of scientific theory and religious belief." Jefferson's deistical science similarly affirmed both.

Recent scientific discoveries themselves cast doubt on the Dar-winist evolutionary theory taught in American public schools and universities. According to standard evolutionary teachings, life has existed on earth for almost 4 billion of its 4.5 billion years. But until about 600 million years ago no organism more complex than bacteria, algae, and single-cell plankton existed. Then, in the early Cambrian period, around 550 million years ago, complex creatures with teeth, tentacles, jaws, and claws appeared in a burst of de-velopment. Standard Darwinism presented this as taking a leisurely 70 million years of gradual evolution.

But recent archaeological finds in China, Greenland, and Siberia show this explosion of new species occurred in a briefer and briefer period: 40 million years, then 30 million years, then 5 million years, now possibly 1 million years. Suddenly the scientific data seem to be supporting a creationist view rather than an evolutionary view. Dr. Stephen Gould of Harvard University remarked, "Now this greatest of evolutionary bursts is even more of an evolutionary burst than we'd thought." The whole Darwinist house of cards may be heading toward collapse. As MIT's Samuel Bowring says, "And what I ask my biologist friends is, 'How fast can evolution get be-fore they start feeling uncomfortable?' "

Jefferson's deistical view, combined with his scientific caution, could have predicted this. He was not a "creationist" in the con-temporary American sense of taking a literal view of the Book of Genesis account, but he believed in an all-knowing Creator of the universe. By running too far ahead of their data, he would have said, evolutionists generalized a theory that later discoveries refuted. And Darwinists turned out to be "monkey's uncles" in more ways than one!

The other great debate of contemporary American science looks *inside* the universe of the human gene rather than outside the universe that mankind exists in. Genetic discovery and engineering foreshadows both great benefits and great dangers. Human genes are being found that predispose individuals to various diseases (cancer, cystic fibrosis, alcoholism) and behavior patterns (violence, daydreaming, overeating) and even intelligence. If those genes can be "corrected," many deadly diseases may be cured and social problems solved.

But ethicists remind us of Nazi Germany's use of eugenics to justify killing or sterilizing social "undesirables" (like the mentally defective or "politically incorrect"). Discrimination against or even punishment of the "genetically unfit" could create another Holocaust. Already, according to the Congressional Office of Technology Assessment, 20 percent of American companies use genetic tests on employees, mostly to hold down corporate health care costs. Insurance companies may unfairly turn down people with high-risk genetic conditions. This potential abuse of individuals' civil liberties would involve Jefferson's scientific caution.

The human "creation" of mutant species would also bring in Jefferson's concern. When University of Pennsylvania researcher Ralph Brinster combined mouse cells with a human gene of growth hormone, producing giant mice, the specter of Dr. Frankensteins loomed before many Americans. Arguing that an obese mouse might help fat people better lose weight, Brinster and many other geneticists resist any controls on scientific research. Science historian Dr. Angela Creager expressed the Jeffersonian balance when she said in the *New York Times,* "Part of what makes science great is freedom of inquiry, but I think there is research that we should really worry about." Jefferson, the most multifaceted scientific mind of early America, would concur, believing that civilized prudence should temper scientific hubris.

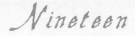

Nineteen

ENTERTAINMENT

*"I had rather be shut up in a very modest cottage, with
my books, my family and a few old friends . . . letting
the world roll on as it liked than to occupy the most
splendid post which any human power can give."*
—THOMAS JEFFERSON, 1788

Jefferson's idea of entertainment revolved around learning and social engagement. Discovery and friendship. Intellectual growth and conversation. Except for his athletic activity (walking and horseback riding), every leisure moment was devoted to either investigation of knowledge or socializing with family and friends. All of these forms of "entertainment" Jefferson found elevating, improving, pleasurable, and contributing to the good life over many years. He preferred these social and intellectual amusements over the noisy and vulgar entertainment of the baser sorts of men: gambling, cockfighting, drunken brawls, wenching and whoring with lower-class and slave women, and loud parties and revelries. For truly satisfying entertainment, of the highest human kind, he recommended "a family for leisure moments, . . . mixed with books, a little letter writing, and neighborly and friendly society . . ." These constitute, for Jefferson, "a plenum of occupation and of happiness which leaves no wish for the noisy and barren amusements and distractions of a city." He preferred home and hearth, field and plain, over court and high society.

Much of Jefferson's ideal entertainment involved the lost art of conversation. Talk not only for the sake of information but for pleasure and mental amusement and relaxation. A visitor from Boston remarked on the master of Monticello's "most gentlemanly and philosophical" conversation. An art and noble entertainment.

Americans have almost totally forgotten this pleasure of gentle conversation. Most verbal expression now, if not totally canned ("Will you have french fries with that?"; "Are you satisfied with your long-distance company?"), degrades the "speaker" and annoys the listener and is purely assertive: forcefully conveying opinion or demanding something. Often, as we see on most television or radio talk shows, it is rude and vulgar—designed to shock and anger, insult and hurt.

Jefferson's idea of conversation was a gentle talk, informed, witty, pleasant—in which knowledge was shared among familiar partners. Relaxing; joyous; satisfying; uplifting. Going away from such a conversation, one feels uplifted, energized, happy. Not worn-out, disgusted, and bored. I admit, I know little of this Jeffersonian conversation, except among a few close friends and family members. And then, we are usually so rushed that it occurs infrequently and is frustratingly short. Our telephone answering machines often know us better than we do ourselves. But I remember my grandparents' home, where this classical conversation occurred regularly. Sitting around together in a comfortable parlor or "screen porch" or back garden, having long, leisurely conversations over refreshments, undisturbed by ringing phones, blaring televisions, humming computers, or beeping pagers. This family and friendly conversation (which still exists in "backward"[!] countries) constituted entertainment, before more sophisticated technological amusements consumed American life. A quieter, more civilized entertainment.

A striking example of this civilized entertainment—conversation among intelligent, thoughtful people—is recorded by a French visitor to Jefferson's home, Monticello. The nobleman, the Marquis de Chastellux, was a member of the French Academy and a major general in Rochambeau's army during the American Revolution. He stayed in Governor Jefferson's home in 1782 and left a delightful description of the Virginian's mountaintop estate and family. He described Jefferson as "tall, and with mild and pleasing countenance . . . whose mind and understanding are ample substitutes for every exterior grace." He found the master of the house a bit distant at first, even formal and cold; but as their acquaintanceship developed, Jefferson became more warm and friendly.

One evening, after everyone had retired, the marquis wandered down from his bedroom to the book-lined library to find Jefferson sitting before the fireplace reading. A punch bowl was on the table nearby, and the master invited the French general to help himself. They sat before the fire and talked until they discovered a shared love of an ancient poet. Long into the night they exchanged favorite quotes from Ossian, giving joy and delight to each other. A memorable evening. And one that proved to the Frenchman that even Americans could be civilized!

This elevated conversation is why Jefferson valued friendship. "The happiest moments my heart knows," he wrote, were those spent with close friends, in intimate and familiar conversation. Not discussing business or self, but learning the character of the other person and learning from it. To St. George Tucker he wrote, "What an ocean is life! And how our barks get separated in beating through it! One of the greatest comforts of the retirement to which I shall soon withdraw will be its rejoining me to my earliest and best friends . . ."

The one thing that made him truly happy was the "frequent society of my friends." With Aristotle, who said that human associations could be based on use, pleasure, or goodness, Jefferson agreed that the truest friendship was only possible between equally noble, intelligent characters, and would endure many changes of fortune. "Friendship is precious, not only in the shade," he said, "but in the sunshine of life." To one of his oldest and best friends, Dr. Benjamin Rush of Philadelphia, Jefferson rhapsodied on an ancient companionship: "I find friendship to be like wine, raw when new, ripened with age, the true old man's milk and restorative cordial." Again like Aristotle, who considered the "reasoned speech" of mankind the distinguishing feature of humanity, Jefferson considered a life without intimate talking friends almost subhuman, or at least a very miserable existence. That's why he tried to persuade all his best friends (James Madison, James Monroe, and William Short) to buy land near Monticello, build their homes near to his, and have a *"partie quarée"* of frequent visits and delightful companionship. Andrew Burstein in his perceptive book *The Inner Jefferson* captures this Jeffersonian sense of friendly entertainment when he writes:

> Friendship is a wonderful mystery of time. It is, in any age, a prime social relation, universally understood to be an important source of entertainment and emotional fulfillment, an intellectual outlet, a desirable instrument for acquiring images of all that exists beyond the self. It can offer a convenient (and sometimes crucial) sounding board for one's own thoughts, more powerful than family by its voluntary nature.

When Jefferson could not be in the immediate presence of his friends, he carried on the conversation in copious letters—which John Adams said had the advantages of conversation but even more depth and profundity. Oh, what Jefferson would have done with e-mail: instantaneous correspondence with his international network of friends; daily "conversation" with friends in France, England, and Russia (back when letters took months or years to arrive!).

After the "entertainment" of friendship, Jefferson's social circle included family (see chapter 6, "Family Values"), where again conversation abounded. A granddaughter recalls playing chess with Jefferson underneath a tall tree in the yard accompanied by witty conversation. Dinner-table conversation. Conversation on leisurely evening walks.

The other main entertainment of the bard of Monticello was reading and scientific discovery (see chapter 18, "Science," for the latter). Gaining knowledge by poring over books. The slave boy Madison Hemings (an alleged son of Jefferson's by Sally Hemings) recounts that "he occupied much of the time in his office engaged in correspondence and reading and writing." He was an avid reader, building a mature library of 6,500 volumes, which became the nucleus of the Library of Congress. How he would enjoy the library of the Internet! He wrote notes in his books' margins, carrying on "conversations" with their authors; he compiled favorite quotes in commonplace notebooks; he composed two books: *Notes on the State of Virginia* and *The Jefferson Bible, or The Morals of Jesus* (compiled from the four Gospels and presented in English, Greek, Latin, and French).

When Jefferson's entertainment wasn't interpersonal, it was informative, intellectual. Elevated. Designed to cultivate the highest faculties in human nature: the mind; the spirit; a refined sense of beauty; appreciation of goodness. As Professor Burstein aptly notes: "Men were attracted to his compelling range as a conversationalist, women to his gentle manner." Social intercourse and the gaining of knowledge were his entertainment.

Contrast this with the $400-billion American entertainment industry. The top category of that entertainment is electronic: VCRs, videotapes, and music recordings. Americans now spend over $100 billion more on entertainment per year than on all elementary and secondary education (public and private). Given that much of this electronic entertainment is on the level of *Beavis and Butthead*, it's no wonder we are a more ignorant, violent, and rude society. In one year the brutally gory video game Mortal Kombat earned $2 billion in revenues (and a $35-million live-action movie followed). Surveys have shown that a typical American teenager watches an average of four "slasher" movies a month (movies that feature bloody murders, cannibalism, rape, and beheadings), and a third of nine-year-olds have viewed at least one sexually violent video. Is it any wonder Generation X is confused, dysfunctional, drug-addicted, and violent? Hollywood and cable TV entertainment has become so sleazy that even some prominent producers (like Clint Eastwood) admit it should be cleaned up. The vulgar entertainment in America degrades the viewer and corrupts our society. And those who produce it are responsible for this national destruction.

But cheer up! The fastest-growing "entertainment" in America is now gambling! From burgeoning state-run lotteries to casinos in Chicago, Boston, and Philadelphia, riverboat gambling in Pittsburgh and Joliet, Illinois, and gambling on Indian reservations, America is becoming one big crap table. And this isn't the horse race and cockfight gambling of Jefferson's day; it is for higher and higher stakes. Bell Atlantic sees a multimillion-dollar new business in gambling through interactive television! Promus Companies, according to a *BusinessWeek* article, is building a chain of Harrah's casinos throughout the country (maybe every McDonald's could have one for parents to amuse themselves while the kiddies jump in the Playland balls).

The sudden surge of gambling in America is explained by investor Richard Rainwater: "It's kind of addicting." It grows by putting people in bondage, destroying families, ruining careers, costing the nation in increased social costs of crime, welfare, and mental health care. This, despite the fact that Atlantic City's gamble with casinos has not provided the promised financial boon. Meanwhile, an airline is testing a machine that allows fliers to play poker on international flights using their credit cards. Most casino jobs are low-paying and high-turnover. Degrading.

Jefferson would find most of current American entertainment corrosive to individual talent and morals and destructive to social well-being. It would remind him of the wealthy, decadent end of the Roman Empire, where less and less worthwhile production and art were thriving and more and more time was spent on watching violent games at the Colosseum (gladiators, naval battles, feeding Christians to lions) and at orgies. Until the "barbarians" were at the gates. And they just marched in and took over (killing a lot of overweight, toga-draped Roman citizens in the bargain). Has anyone checked the Mexican army lately?

Thomas Jefferson's idea of entertainment as civilized conversation and intellectual pursuits seems old-fashioned and quaint today. But his belief in the value of uplifting, healthy, and improving leisure activities is echoed by Mark Landler, a writer on the media: "Television . . . has already turned us into a nation of empty vessels—reliant on TV for the emotional and intellectual sustenance that families and society used to provide . . . Will entertainment rob us of whatever imagination we have left?"

A *BusinessWeek* article on the booming entertainment industry could have been quoting T. J. himself when it said, "Even more innocent forms of entertainment—consumed in great quantities—may deprive us of the chance to enrich ourselves through reading, conversation, or real experiences that haven't been filtered and packaged as entertainment commodities." Still, one can imagine Jefferson savoring much of PBS's civilized fare, as well as intellectual channels like Discovery, A&E, and the History Channel.

Besides the 2.5 million people who work directly in the entertainment industry, the "entertainment ethic" increasingly pervades all other aspects of American life. Politics now relies on candidates looking good on TV (culminating in movie actor President Ronald Reagan); Dads are supposed to be "fun"; even college professors are evaluated by students on a TV rating–style system (requiring them to use Johnny Carson one-liners or in-class videos); news programs look more and more like Hollywood fluff and grocery store scandal sheets.

Thomas Jefferson would be saddened by all this. He might think this American lust to be constantly entertained and amused was a sign of social trivia and decline. Worse, the need for greater and greater stimulation would indicate to him a desire for meaning in life that such vulgar and perverse entertainment cannot satisfy. The joy he had in leisure activities around close friends, family, conversation, learning, and faith did satisfy true human needs for growth—intellectual and spiritual. The saddest thing about American schlock entertainment is that it doesn't entertain. It leaves an empty taste, a dissatisfaction that true human activity fulfills. The increasing frenzy for more and wilder entertainment only feeds itself, until it ends in disappointment and death.

Conclusion

"LIFE, LIBERTY AND HAPPINESS": JEFFERSON'S HOPES FOR AMERICA

"I sincerely pray that all the members of the human family may, in the time prescribed by the Father of us all, find themselves securely established in the enjoyments of life, liberty and happiness."

—THOMAS JEFFERSON, 1807

Thomas Jefferson had many interesting hopes for America. For example, he hoped that someday Cuba would become a state. Imagine, Cuba as the fifty-first state of the United States of America! Maybe Castro could be its first senator! Or Jesse Jackson!

Actually, Jefferson's greatest hope was that an intelligent American citizenry would elect the "natural aristocracy" for political leadership in Washington and the state capitals and enjoy the blessings of freedom, happiness, peace, prosperity, and justice. The political aristocracy of "virtue and talents" rather than the "pseudo-aristocracy" of wealth or fame. Jefferson hoped that an active, intelligent electorate would see their interest best served by such men, "the best" ruling, and show them respect and honor. The cynical attitudes Americans have toward politics and political leaders would disappoint Jefferson.

George F. Will shares Jefferson's concern for public cynicism, capturing it in the equation $R = C^2$ (realism equals cynicism squared). He cites reasons for this corrosive tendency in the American polity like Congress's "baseline budgeting"—a sneaky technique to show "cuts" in the federal budget while increasing spending. He likens it to eating five pounds of Thanksgiving turkey this year and enjoying it so much that you pledge to eat ten pounds of turkey next Thanksgiving. On reflection you scale that back to six pounds and claim a 40 percent reduction in your gluttony! Then, as Clinton did to Dole, accuse your opponents of threatening to "cut" your turkey allowance to only five and a half pounds!

George Will concludes that today's politicians divide their time between decrying national cynicism and doing things that deepen that cynicism. He's right. The term "Watergate" becomes modified to symbolize the latest political scandal, like "FBI-gate" in the Clinton administration (or "Bimbo-gate" for Bill) and "Rubbergate" for congressional members' habit of bouncing checks (without penalty) in the House Bank.

Meg Greenfield doesn't see contemporary American cynicism any different from that in the past (Mark Twain or Will Rogers, for example) and even finds it a bit healthy. From the ancient Greek meaning of the word, she sees it as "disillusionment, disbelief, skepticism and inclination not to take things at face value." Such an attitude is an accurate assessment of the human propensity to want cake and eat it too; even the highest members of the government, church, and corporations to succumb to temptation and fall. Or ordinary citizens to practice the hypocrisy of demanding big cuts in the federal budget and taxes but maintaining federal programs that benefit them. Hence the old joke from the phrase on American money: "In God we trust—all others pay cash." But this Augustinian view of untrustworthy, fallen humanity—prone to sin (and then lie about it)—was more characteristic of the Puritans than Jefferson. He had an Enlightenment and classical optimism about mankind's capacity for improvement and virtue. He may have been disappointed a lot by the end of his life, but he never abandoned his hope that through education, economic equality, political awareness, and a common ethic, we might build a kind of "heaven on earth" in the United States.

So, first, Jefferson would hope that talented, dedicated men would make the sacrifice (and he knew it is a sacrifice—of one's privacy, wealth, and ease) to go into politics. Not out of love of money, fame, or attention, but out of a love of country and sense of duty. Jefferson risked losing his fortune and his life by entering politics during the American Revolution. Had we lost the Revolutionary War, T. J. might have found himself hanging from a London gallows.

Who among the current national leadership constitutes that Jeffersonian quality? Clinton? Gingrich? Kemp? I'm not sure Jefferson would be wildly enthusiastic about any of them. And the system of humiliating primaries, journalistic exposés, and public ridicule that keeps the best leaders from considering politics would deeply disturb Jefferson. Few intelligent, self-respecting people consider the masochism of going into American politics.

But Jefferson hoped that with an intelligent electorate and enlightened leadership, we could all enjoy "life, liberty and happiness" in America. As Gary Amos in his book *Defending the Declaration* said of Jefferson's original use of this phrase in 1776: "By 1776 the colonists finally realized that it was useless to depend on their 'rights as Englishmen' before the king and Parliament. So in the Declaration, they appealed to a higher standard of rights—'unalienable rights' endowed by the Creator. These were rights ordained by God . . . conferred by a higher king than King George . . ."

Life

"Life" in Jefferson's time was almost as prominent a concept as it is in our late-twentieth-century America (with "pro-life," "right to life," "quality of life," and the pope's encyclical *The Gospel of Life*). Jefferson was most familiar with two statements of the importance of life: John Locke's famous phrase in *The Second Treatise of Government* (which informed the Declaration of Independence) that all humans have natural rights to "*Life,* Liberty and Property"; and the Gospel of John (3:16): "For God so loved the world, that he gave his only begotten Son, that whosoever believeth in him should not perish, but have everlasting *life*" (emphasis mine). Jefferson summarizes the former as "We hold these truths to be sacred and undeniable; that all men are created equal and independent, that from that equal creation they derive rights inherent and inalienable, among which are the preservation of *life,* and liberty and the pursuit of happiness . . ." (emphasis mine).

Life for Jefferson means both prosperity and freedom. "Affectionate concerns for the prosperity of my fellow citizens will cease but with life to animate my breast," he said. America is the most economically prosperous nation in the history of the world. One only has to visit other countries to realize how prosperous we are. This material prosperity has flowed from our mixed economic system of private enterprise (which encourages invention and rewards creativity and hard work) and social welfare (which nourishes equal opportunity and helps the truly needy). Jefferson advocated such a mixed system. The trick is keeping the right balance. Since the 1930s we've seen the problems of excessive social welfare and regulation; but going back to pure laissez-faire capitalism will not work either. "Downsizing" has about had it in the U.S. economy. Jefferson would admire leaders who are both sensible and sensitive, balancing private enterprise with public services. The benefit of the two-party system in America is that it keeps a balance between the two extremes of socialist statism and capitalist individualism and greed.

With economic prosperity assured, Jefferson would want Americans to go on to higher things: morals, charity, goodness, service. These qualities are best developed in an atmosphere of freedom: freedom of speech and press, freedom of religion, and freedom of association. But to do any of these things, one has to be alive. Living.

Jefferson's emphasis on "life" seems hauntingly relevant today, as Americans debate abortion, capital punishment, and euthanasia. America's concern with the sanctity of life animates much of our history, long before Pope John Paul II criticized the West for its "culture of death." The Civil War struggle over slavery was often couched in terms of that institution stealing the "life" of the slave.

Several commentators have compared the emotional divisiveness of the abortion debate to the slavery controversy in the early 1800s. Even this, however, has reached a strange consensus along Jeffersonian lines. Both the pro-choice advocates who insist on a woman's right to an abortion and the pro-life advocates who want to outlaw all abortions couch their arguments in terms of life. Pro-choice leaders decry extremists murdering abortion doctors and bombing abortion clinics. Pro-life bumper stickers read, "Thank God Your Mother Was Pro-Life" and "I'm for the Rights of Unborn Women," countered by pro-choice bumper stickers saying, "I'm Pro-Choice and Pro-Child/Only Wanted Babies" or "If You're Against Abortion, Don't Have One" (echoing the South's argument "If you don't like slavery don't own slaves—but leave ours alone!"). President Clinton, the Great Compromiser, wants abortion "safe, legal and rare." Even the review of the book *Lovejoy: A Year in the Life of an Abortion Clinic* in the *New York Times Book Review* by Meryl Gordon admitted discomfort over the cutting up of fetal organs for medical research.

Jefferson's law against abortion (or "saticide") reflects the emerging American consensus that this tragedy harms the woman as much as the preborn (as a parent's affection for children is the strongest in nature). This commends an equal sympathy for the woman as for the fetus. The guilt and remorse of millions of women who have had abortions commends a notion of the possibility of forgiveness, if this American tragedy is ever to get behind us. A French "abortion pill" isn't the answer either; its "convenience," like high-tech warfare, makes the act all the more horrifying. For Jefferson, ease of action would ultimately compound the crime and guilt.

On the other contemporary challenge to life, the "mercy killing" of the sick and aged—a la "Dr. Death" Jack Kevorkian—whose "assisted suicides" have spawned a contemporary controversy almost equal to the abortion issue, Jefferson would again share sympathy with both sides. At times he suffered the debilitating effects of old age and illness and expressed to John Adams that he looked forward to meeting his Maker. He detested the infirmities of old age. Upon seeing Charles Thompson (a signer of the Declaration of Independence) at age ninety-three, Jefferson was horrified to find this once intelligent, vigorous man "cheerful, slender as a grasshopper, and so much without memory that he scarcely recognizes the members of his household." Alzheimer's. Even Jefferson asked, "Is this life?" And he replied, "It is at most the life of a cabbage . . ." A vegetable. But he didn't go on to suggest squashing that cabbage, putting Thompson "out of his misery," just as no one I know has suggested putting Alzheimer's sufferer Ronald Reagan out of his misery (some would have liked to during his presidency!).

Socially sanctioned suicide would violate Jefferson's notion of natural law in which one neither interrupts life artificially (euthanasia) nor prolongs it artificially (such as with forced feeding or artificial lungs). Despite his physical sufferings near the end of his life, Jefferson never suggested suicide as the answer. And the potential for abuse of such a social policy would terrify Jefferson.

As a large, aging baby boomer generation enters senior citizenhood (and unproductivity), the temptation to "relieve them of their suffering" (and society of their burden) seems a bit macabre for a civilized country. The Nazi Holocaust made a similar case not only against Jews but against socialists, homosexuals, and the mentally retarded. A society that rationalizes the killing of the most outcast or vulnerable members of its population cannot be called civilized in any Jeffersonian meaning of the term. Human life soon loses its value. Jefferson's acquaintance with Scripture may have reminded him of two other times when young life was murdered: Pharaoh killing all newborn Hebrew boys (Moses only escaping in a basket on the Nile) and Herod ordering the killing of all baby boys two years old and under in Bethlehem.

The most hopeful sign of this issue of "life" for Jefferson would be that Americans still take it seriously enough to get upset. In most of Europe issues of abortion, euthanasia, and capital punishment, and homosexuality have all been settled (along the lines of acceptance) and are not even discussed anymore. That's why Europe still regards the United States as quaint and puritanical. Jefferson would say we still have our conscience intact. There's hope.

Liberty

Liberty for Jefferson meant more than just being free to do what you want. It meant a disciplined pursuit of goodness and happiness. And "the liberty of speaking and writing guards our other liberties." So those who advance freedom to do selfish, evil, or immoral things are not consistent with Jefferson. He hoped freedom of economic activity would produce the most prosperity; freedom of speech and press would produce the most wisdom; and freedom of religion the most moral society. Its fruits.

Which groups and causes in America today are contributing to that kind of freedom? One example is the men's group Promise Keepers, which emphasizes men's responsibility to women and families and communities. In a *New York Times* article on this organization, which has no officers or official membership, the members of a diverse group of American men (white and black, rich and poor, short-haired and long-haired, but mostly in their thirties and forties) pledge to take responsibility for their actions. Its founder was quoted as saying, "Leadership is servanthood, for the guy to be the leader means he outserves his wife." Strong, stable families are Promise Keepers' goal. Responsibility. Integrity.

Happiness

Jefferson wrote his young ward Peter Carr a classic prescription for personal happiness: "Health, learning and virtue will insure your happiness; they will give you a quiet conscience, private esteem and public honor." He would prescribe the same formula for America's social happiness: a healthy society both physically and morally; a learned society through education, thought, and reflection; and a virtuous society, reviving the decency, charity, and discipline of our past. Recognizing and confessing our faults; striving for a better America. Again, one only has to visit other countries or entertain foreign guests to realize how "puritanically" moral America still is. Jefferson was shocked by the decadence of Europe and he still would be. He also would see peace as essential to happiness. "Always a friend to peace and believing it to promote eminently the happiness and prosperity of nations . . ." And peace for Jefferson is not possible without justice: "Peace and justice should be the polar stars of the American societies," he wrote. Happiness is the most important of all social goods, for Jefferson, and he said, "Without virtue, happiness cannot be."

His final hope for America would be for a happiness through virtue. Again, Jefferson predicts the future, or at least, the American psyche. Both political parties put forward "virtue" as essential in America during the last presidential campaign. Democrats through Clinton's talk of "responsibility" and Republicans through traditional moral, "family" issues. This reflects general American concern with declining social order. Howard Fineman in *Newsweek* correctly observed that "the fraying of America's social fabric—once considered the crotchety preoccupation of the cultural right—has become a national (even liberal) obsession."

The "Virtuecrats" like William Bennett articulate a universal American belief that there are accepted principles of good character, and society is no longer teaching them. A recent survey showed that 76 percent of Americans believe that "the United

States is in moral and spiritual decline." During the 1996 campaign, candidates at town meetings got questions on civility, decency, and respect as much as on the economy and foreign affairs. Asked who's to blame for this "virtue-gate," a poll showed that 77 percent said the breakdown of the family, 76 percent said individuals themselves, 67 percent said television and popular entertainment, and 55 percent said government leaders.

Jefferson's notion of virtue was equally derived from classical Greek philosophy (Aristotle)—a kind of public-spirited concern for others—and Judeo-Christian moral standards (charity, reverence, forbearance, forgiveness, etc.). Looking at the popular vices of America—greed, adultery, murder, drugs and gambling addiction, and violence—he would probably agree with Michael Horowitz, who said: "if we are serious about this, it means we will have to sacrifice some measure of freedom we now have to do anything we want if it feels good." Or as Fineman states: "In the end, it's not the laws we pass but the lives we lead." It requires a change in the individual. Jefferson would concur. And he would be hopeful that we can attain it if we look ahead with promise, not back at past wrongs.

AUTHOR BIOGRAPHY

DR. GARRETT WARD SHELDON received a Ph.D. from Rutgers University, New Brunswick. He has lectured on Jeffersonian Democracy at Oxford University, Moscow University, the University of Virginia, and Trinity Divinity School.

Professor Sheldon's first book on Jefferson, *The Political Philosophy of Thomas Jefferson* (Johns Hopkins University Press), was the first American book on Jefferson to be translated into Russian and published in Moscow (1996). He has assisted a scholar in India on a book dealing with Jefferson and Gandhi. He is now commissioned by the government of Turkey to write a volume on Jefferson and Ataturk. Scholars in England, Russia, Hungary, and the Middle East have consulted Sheldon in their Jefferson studies.

Dr. Sheldon is the John Morton Beaty Professor of Political and Social Science at Clinch Valley College of the University of Virginia. In 1992 he won the Outstanding Faculty in Virginia Award.